POWER PLAYS

POWER PLAYS

Politics, Football, and Other Blood Sports

JOHN M. BARRY

University Press of Mississippi Jackson

Publication of this book was made possible in
part by Wood and Jane Hiatt, Hiatt-Ingram Fund
of the Greater Jackson Foundation

www.upress.state.ms.us

09 08 07 06 05 04 03 02 01   4 3 2 1

∞

Library of Congress Cataloging-in-Publication Data

Barry, John M., 1947–

  Power plays : politics, football, and other blood sports / John M. Barry.

    p.   cm.

  ISBN 1-57806-404-X (cloth : alk. paper)

    1. United States—Politics and government—1989–   2. Power (Social
sciences)—United States—History—20th century.   3. Political corruption—
United States—History—20th century.   4. Football—Social aspects—United
States—History—20th century.   5. Sports—Social aspects—United States—
History—20th century.   6. Politicians—United States—Biography.

7. Athletes—United States—Biography.   I. Title.

E839.5.B39 2001

303.3'0973—dc21   2001026659

British Library Cataloging-in-Publication Data available

To Lawrence Renaldo Lopes,
who was Jimmy

age 23, 101st airborne,
casualty type A1 hostile, died,
reason: multiple fragmentation wounds,
The Wall Panel 46E-Row 047

CONTENTS

HOME   1

Flexible Blocking Patterns   3

Jimmy   11

WASHINGTON: THE PLAYERS   19

The Making of a Politician I   21

The Making of a Politician II   35

The Media   45

GAME'S OVER   55

It's All a Part of the Game   57

No More Play   65

Regrets   80

WASHINGTON: WRIGHT'S PLAY   83

The Floor   85

Peace   93

The Vote   99

WASHINGTON: GINGRICH'S PLAY   131

The Outside Game   133

THE OLYMPIANS   151

Renaldo Nehemiah   153

Linda Dragan   158

Michael Storm   163

Mark Cameron   168

Postscript   175

THE FALL   177

The Trial   179

Epilogue   203

Index   211

HOME

The great political process was not begun by the worker, the intellectual, the priest, properly speaking, or the business-man, but by youth, preoccupied with women and resolved to fight—the lover, the warrior, the athlete.

—JOSÉ ORTEGA Y GASSET

FLEXIBLE BLOCKING PATTERNS

Everything in this book means something personal to me, including the title of this chapter. The first story that I ever sold was initially titled "Flexible Blocking Patterns." At the time I was a football coach, and the story explained to other coaches how a team could call its blocking assignments at the last second, after it broke the huddle and lined up, to take advantage of a weakness in the defense or to avoid a disaster. The story ran in *Scholastic Coach* magazine. The editor in his wisdom changed the title, but now at least I get to use it to title this chapter. It seems more appropriate here anyway.

"Flexible Blocking Patterns" represents ways in which we attempt to maneuver to exploit openings or avoid disasters. How we adjust, twist, block. How we try to survive and, sometimes, strike and conquer. For a block is not defensive merely; in football one *throws* a block, and it is an offensive, attacking move. In other words, the title represents ways in which all of us try to exercise power.

This book explores that exercise of power. It is a collection. Some of the pieces in here are new, but most have appeared either in a magazine or in my first book. All of them examine how power works.

Some, those about politics, do so in an obvious way. Others, particularly those about athletes, do so less obviously. But all look at the price one pays to win, the price of losing, how one imposes one's will on others (a process that usually begins with imposing one's will on oneself), and how people react when the world grinds slowly away at them, when the world grinds exceeding small.

Even in my days as a coach I wondered about such things, about how power can be used or abused, not only in the abstract or en masse but in individual relationships. I wondered as well about force, dominion, might, sovereignty, rule, authority, and how those aspects or synonyms of power affect the shape of society. In fact the words themselves can shape the world; George Orwell made that point long before the fashion of deconstruction. So the words themselves can matter.

Sport analogies are often applied to politics, and for that matter to war. This makes at least some sense: in sports and in politics the competitiveness, the dedication to a goal, the abilities of particular individuals, and in many instances team effort all play a role in determining who wins and who loses. And of course the British victory over Napoleon was said to have been determined on the playing fields of Eton.

Indeed, the connections between sport and politics may go even deeper. As already noted, José Ortega y Gasset argued, "The great political process was not begun by the worker, the intellectual, the priest, properly speaking, or the businessman, but by youth, preoccupied with women and resolved to fight—the lover, the warrior, the athlete."

And for me the connection between sport and politics is tied quite directly to my work. Had I not coached football, I would not have been able to write my first book. Which is odd, considering the subject.

In that book I wanted to analyze how power works in Washington. At the time I was a journalist covering national politics. I preferred writing a narrative, a case study, to some static analysis. The case study I chose turned out to be better for my purpose than I could have hoped, better in fact than I wished it to be. It turned out to be the story of the destruction of one man who had spent his life in politics, and the rise to power of another. When Jim Wright became Speaker of the U.S. House of Representatives I asked him to grant me access to his private meetings. I told Wright the book would use his effort to control policy and move legislation as a narrative vehicle to describe the exercise of power.

When I asked him to grant me access, he barely knew me, and he had a far worse relationship with the press than did most politicians—and none of them like the press, or truly have a good relationship with it. I had met him for the first time only a few weeks before making my request, when I began working on a profile of him for the *New York Times Magazine.* Yet he gave me more than I asked for—much more—allowing me into virtually all his meetings during his speakership. If any staff attended a meeting, I could attend, with nothing off the record. I believed at the time, and Wright later confirmed, that he agreed to cooperate because his first ambition in life was to be a football coach and I had coached football. Because of that he saw me as different from other journalists, thought of me as someone who might understand him better.

His nemesis Newt Gingrich also cooperated with me, as did others among Wright's allies and enemies, but they would not have done so had Wright not already granted me such extraordinary access.

As it turned out, Wright served only two and a half years as Speaker—he became the first Speaker in history forced to resign. Still, he was a remarkable man who even in that short term did remarkable things. Gingrich achieved power by destroying him.

The cooperation of both Wright, a constitutional officer who wielded power from the dais above the floor—the dais from which the president gives the state of the union address each year—and Gingrich, then a back bencher with no formal leadership position of any kind in his party, meant that I observed first-hand the events leading to Wright's auto-da-fe. The most difficult thing I have ever done as a writer was to try to maintain distance from and perspective on those events.

The book that came out of those experiences, *The Ambition and the Power: A True Story of Washington*, chronicled more than just the story of Wright's undoing or Gingrich's rise. It detailed the end of the old style of politics and the emergence of the new, a new that has largely held sway since. Indeed, Bill Kovach, who has served as Washington bureau chief of the *New York Times*, editor of the *Atlanta Constitution*, and curator of the Nieman Foundation, reviewed the book and noted that it "may presage the final push for political dominance in Washington."

That book's sales disappointed not only me—no surprise, all writers think their books will become bestsellers—but also my editor, who had a more realistic grasp on marketing realities, and it went out of print a few years later. With perfect irony, almost the day it went out of print, the *New York Times Book Review* listed it as one of the eleven best books ever written on the ways of Washington and Congress. (Why the *Times* listed a "top eleven" instead of a "top ten" I have always wondered, but I'm not complaining.) Gingrich himself called it one of the three best books ever written on Congress; his other favorites are Woodrow Wilson's *Congressional Government* and Allen Drury's novel *Advise and Consent*. Wright embraced the book as well. That these two most bitter antagonists both considered the book accurate and fair meant something to me.

Sport, politics, and war are said to be all about winning. War is of course about nothing but winning and has no rules, and, as the Wright-Gingrich contest shows, politics can be almost as brutal, but I have never believed that sports are about only winning. My somewhat heretical view on this—heretical at least for an ex-football coach—stems not from any lack of competitive zeal, but from the belief that winning by itself is superficial. Maybe my feelings in this area come from my own experience not in football but in individual sports, high school track and field and competitive weightlifting after college.

At Classical High School in Providence, Rhode Island, my football and track coach was Al Morro, who had been an NCAA champion in the discus and captain of a Boston College football team ranked in the top five nationally. Al is an unusual man, to say the least. Never married, quite mysterious to his players, he coached in the old style. He never swore. The worst thing he ever called someone was "a dirty lousy louse." But getting called that made you feel as low as anything in the world. Sometimes he hit his players, although never with a closed fist. Sometimes he grabbed our face masks and twisted our heads around. Once he warned us, "No matter how hard you get hit out there on the field, you *know* you'll get hit harder in the locker room at half-time." In track he was almost as intense. He sounds like a horrible man. And yet most of his players loved him. I certainly did. And he loved us. He taught us we could give more than we believed we had. He also took care of players who got in trouble with the police, took care of players who had to work to keep their families going, took care of players who needed to be taken care of.

He hated "baloney." Every football team I have ever seen, from the pee-wee level to the pros, counts cadence when it does warm-up exercises, growling, "One-two-three-four! One-two-three-four!" The players' voices rumble up from deep inside their chests, as they try to intimidate the opponent and submerge themselves in a blood-lust.

Not Classical High School. We never counted cadence at all, never made grunting or growling noises, never relied on group-think. When we went through our warm-ups some of us would be stretching our hamstrings, others would be doing jumping jacks, others loosening their shoulders.

Oh, Al could get us up. Once we played what he considered one of the best teams in New England, a team far better than we were, and he got us so psyched we didn't just beat them, we absolutely took them apart. That was probably the only game I've ever been involved in when emotion utterly overwhelmed talent. But also once, as we left the locker room really psyched, ready to kill the other team, we shouted, "Let's GO!"

Al turned around and said, "Oh yeah? Where ya going?"

Deflated, thrown off, we lost that game.

I guess he preferred each of us to ready himself alone, to face the world alone. Not that he didn't believe and work toward creating a harmonious team, but we are alone in the world and he knew that.

In track, he was a truly great field event coach. In a mid-sized public high school that did not recruit athletes and sent practically every graduate to a four-year college, he produced high school All-Americans. I picked up a *Track and Field News* a few years ago and noticed that in one event, the hammer throw, he had coached seven of the top twenty high school performers of all time, including one athlete who held the teenage world record—an extraordinary feat considering that Russians and Germans have dominated this event for decades. (Alvin Jackson, the athlete who set that record, would soon play on the offensive line for Penn State and bragged he could out-eat anyone; Al Morro took up that particular challenge and trounced him in an eating contest.) His formula for success was simple: hard work and outstanding technique. His field event men—especially shot putters, discus throwers, and so forth—practiced seven days a week, including Easter Sunday.

So maybe because of Al and track, I always thought that even in football you competed chiefly against yourself. Just to score more points than another team? What did that mean? It seemed stupid. Because no matter how bad you are, you can always find some team somewhere you could beat 30–0, and no matter how good you are, some team somewhere is capable of beating you 30–0. So what did the win itself mean? Nothing.

Competing against yourself, to play at your best, that meant something. The difference is akin to that between pride and dignity. Dignity is an internal thing, and it is a kind of truth; it reflects a concern with how one sees one's own self. Pride is something external, and therefore superficial and false; the proud worry about how the world sees them. Pride represents a state of action and aggressiveness, yet people with pride can be manipulated. (It's rather like judo—using an aggressor's own power against him—and not particularly difficult.) Dignity is essentially passive, a state of being. Yet it is also rooted and firm and unyielding, and the more it is tested or assaulted, the stronger and truer it becomes.

My own experience in weightlifting may also have had something to do with my feelings. I was a decent lifter, and if I had trained elsewhere, I might even have considered myself pretty good. At my very best I was capable of qualifying to compete at the national championships. But I was never good enough to contend for a medal there, and I trained at the Central Falls Weightlifting Club in Rhode Island, so I could have no illusions about my abilities. The coach there, Joe Mills, had himself been a national champion and developed the greatest American lifter of the past several decades, Bob Bednarski, a world heavyweight champion who set more than twenty world records. Bednarski, the only American lifter in more than thirty years to win a world championship, was no accident. Mills also produced another lifter who won five straight national heavyweight championships and a bronze medal in the world championships, another man who lifted a national record over his head but couldn't hold it, and still another who set a teenage world record. I was never going to beat any of them, and so I had to compete against myself or why bother lifting at all?

I quit coaching football in fact when the wins, per se, began to matter to me more than anything else. I was on the staff of a nationally ranked and bowl-bound Tulane University team, and we beat one team 42–0. It may have been our worst game of the season, we just completely outclassed them on ability, and yet I kind of liked the idea of playing them just to get the victory and pad our record, instead of testing ourselves against Notre Dame or Michigan or Miami. It meant nothing and I knew that, but I was becoming corrupted. One can have neither pride nor dignity if one is corrupt. So I quit.

I had already started writing and turned to it full-time, went to Washington to cover politics, then left journalism to finish my first book. There is much in subsequent chapters about the media, and I consider reporters to be different from writers. (That distinction is by no means automatically pejorative, but it does exist: a journalist reports what someone else does; a writer creates something new.) But let me say that I think a football coach, a politician committed to doing something real, and a writer resemble each other—at least the good ones do—in three ways. In fact, the same traits can be found to a greater or lesser degree in the best people in most professions where some kind of over-all vision matters.

First they notice ... everything. Henry James urged that a writer "be one of those on whom nothing is lost." Good politicians, coaches, and writers do notice everything. Yet they also focus; while remaining aware of the external, they practice "concentration without elimination," as T. S. Eliot said.

Second, each sits at the center of chaos and, through vision and will, tries to order that chaos. This vision and will function like a crystal to precipitate an order out of possibilities that already exist.

Third, politicians and coaches perform and maneuver, or manipulate, others into performing. A writer too—a good writer does anyway, whether by intent or not—alters the perceptions of others, in turn changing what they do.

Other than that, these professions share little. Politics and coaching are ultimately pure act; writing, pure shadow. A writer simply observes, although he or she is no mere spectator, oh no, as Heisenberg hypothesized, observations have effect. Politics and coaching are entirely social, with success dependent upon how one interacts with others; writing is entirely isolating, with success independent of others. In the former, you are surrounded and involved with many people, sometimes tens of thousands of people. As a writer, you work alone. You see no one in the course of your work. Every eighteen months (if you work fast and I don't) you send something off to your editor. And sometimes you become even more isolated than writing itself demands.

As for me personally, considering the different roles a football coach and a writer play, it may be appropriate that those who know me as one have difficulty picturing me as the other. As a coach, I loved having a sense of certainty of what a team needed to do, loved being at the center, controlling, directing, demanding, manipulating, loved the decisiveness required, the idea of making a decision and making it work. Yet my natural inclination is to observe. I am uncomfortable in crowds, hanging back, more asocial than antisocial.

I quit coaching twenty years ago. I miss not only the game itself, but also the kind of chaos that went with it, and the way one could create something more or less concrete.

But I'm a writer. That's all I ever really wanted to do or be. Write. Maybe the real reason I left football was just because it was time to go home. Home was my writing.

And as the next chapter shows, home is also where I learned my first lesson in real power.

JIMMY

We were never really friends...

Jimmy was not his name but it will do; even now I don't want to intrude on his privacy. He was black. I first met him at John Howland School, the elementary school, on Cole Avenue on the East Side of Providence, Rhode Island. My neighborhood was and is the wealthiest part of the city, the home of intellectuals—Brown University faculty (those who have been around for a while and bought before the real estate values rose)—lawyers, doctors, the people who make shopping trips to New York and adorn their coffee tables with unread *New Yorkers*. The people who say "The Hill" and mean College Hill, home of Brown, when everyone else in the city knows there is only one Hill, Federal Hill, with its narrow streets of five-story wooden tenements where all the Italians lived when they first came to this country.

Ethnically, then as now, the East Side was dominated by Yankees and Jews, with some Irish thrown in.

But that was the "nice" East Side. There was also the "not-so-nice" East Side, the area the *New Yorker* subscribers waved away like some particularly grotesque Koren cartoon or Borges story. The not-so-nice East Side ran in my childhood south of Pitman Street—the Portuguese area called Fox Point—and west of Camp Street, which was black and has since then largely been eliminated by the "slum-clearing" University Heights development.

By this strange quirk, John Howland Elementary School (which itself has been converted into condos), the first school of so many who went on to Brown and Dartmouth and then Yale Law School and Harvard Medical School, was integrated. Not much, mind you, but just enough so that a black face or the name "Ferreira," drawn from the fringes of the school's boundaries, provided the Arnolds and Goldsteins with an early egalitarian experience. Still, one was never much aware of those names and faces; they seemed rarely to say anything in class, almost as if they weren't there, except for the overheard shouts from the (snicker-snicker) Ungraded Room.

Jimmy was not in the Ungraded Room, though I never did know just what class he actually was in. I was in the third grade when I first met him, and Jimmy just seemed to be always around the school, like the graham crackers and milk they gave out in kindergarten. Of course he was older and bigger than I, and of course I was afraid of him, not so much because of his age or size, but because of his strangeness.

Back at John Howland, the lines between the nice and not-so-nice East Siders appeared clearly at lunch. School broke from noon to one, and there was no cafeteria. The nice East Siders went home to eat. The others did not; instead, they swarmed the booths and counter in the luncheonette at Hall's on Elmgrove Avenue. Even then I knew that it wasn't that their mothers cared less for them, but that they lived on the fringes of the neighborhood and had too little time to walk home, eat, and return. Nice East Siders who lived far away were met by mothers in cars at lunchtime. Mothers drove no second cars in the other families.

I lived on an alternate route to Hall's, and ensconced behind my windows, I used to watch the daily pilgrimage. I learned that some of the not-so-nice East Siders took buses home after school, by themselves. It would be years before I could go on a bus alone. I wondered about their freedom, even envied it. I began to eat quickly, then hurry the two blocks to Hall's and join them. Many of my classmates would still be there, a few having hamburgers, but most ordering only a Coke or "cabinet"— what Rhode Islanders, unique in the United States, call milkshakes—to drink with the sandwiches brought from home. Sometimes I would have a Coke too.

Indirectly, my acquaintanceship with Jimmy stemmed from these Cokes, although I had no contact with him at Hall's. I had become mildly friendly with some of the not-so-nice East Siders, one of whom was a friend of Jimmy's, and I frequently walked back to school with them. Often we passed my house. I had always considered it modest, but they marveled at it and called me a liar when I insisted just my one family lived there.

A few days after that accusation I took them inside, up to my room, and displayed my electric trains. Lionel. I was ready to defend them against allegations that American Flyer made superior trains, but my guests gawked without comment and we left. My mother had welcomed us with a distraught look, although she offered everyone snacks. Nothing was ever said, but I did not bring those boys home again. They weren't really friends anyway; I had brought them out of friendliness, but I had patronized them. Years later, when I saw in the paper that one had graduated from the University of Rhode Island I thought, isn't that nice.

I never patronized Jimmy. For one thing, Jimmy was the John Howland bully. At the time I thought that was the only reason he came to school as often as he did—he liked running things. And it isn't true that standing up to a bully forces him to back down. Jimmy didn't back down, he beat down. He had other moments though, when he seemed tired, and he smiled a lot. His smiles were not sadistic ones, but the innocent and curious kind that in an infant fill everyone who sees them with joy.

Often at recess he abdicated his role of bully and sauntered into an area called the "rough"—an area of the schoolyard prohibited to all children because it was littered with rocks and broken glass and was out of the teachers' line of vision, with part of it hidden by a corner of the building. I used to sneak into the rough myself—Jimmy sauntered, I snuck—and we would be alone there. We eyed each other cautiously at first, but soon got used to each other and went about our own independent business.

My first real contact with Jimmy came in the fourth or fifth grade when we became allies, or, more accurately, he became my ally. Another boy in school, the son of one of Providence's unsuccessful mayoralty candidates, and I had a somewhat strange relationship—close friends from April through November, bitter enemies through the winter. He and I led rival factions—were we older, the "factions" might have been called "gangs"—and we had it out each snowstorm. Hard, heavy iceballs were our most common weapons, along with occasional fists and, when things got serious, snowballs with rock centers. These encounters were not playful romps in the snow, but intense grim struggles.

One day rumors swept my faction that the other side had escalated; they would be using not only rock-cores, but thirteen-year-olds. The fear built during the day, deservedly so. The teenagers routed us, scattering us in isolated pockets of ones and twos down Wayland Avenue. I and a few of my lieutenants were stalked and beaten. One of those lieutenants was a not-so-nice East Sider who had been in my house. Through him, and counting on the tolerance that had developed between us in the rough, I approached Jimmy for help. The teenagers were dealt with.

I left John Howland for Nathan Bishop Junior High School, and saw Jimmy only twice more. At John Howland I had skipped three grades; at Nathan Bishop I entered the city's first accelerated program, three years condensed to two. I don't remember Jimmy at Bishop. He must have gone to another junior high, with different neighborhood boundaries and no more contact with the Yankees and Jews who attended John Howland. I was continuing in my East Side tradition—even to seeing a psychiatrist, quite *avant garde* back then, because of what was termed "violent anti-social behavior"—and Jimmy was continuing in his East Side tradition.

I ran into Jimmy two years later, a few weeks before leaving Bishop for—where else?—Classical High School. Classical was a public school technically open to anyone in the city, but it focused intensively on academics. Roughly 20 percent of my high school graduating class went to either Ivy League schools or places like Stanford, Chicago, and Swarthmore, and only a single boy in my class did not go to a four-year college; he joined the Marines instead.

It was May when I saw Jimmy, a beautiful spring day. I had returned to John Howland to visit Margaret Toole, my favorite teacher at the time and the favorite of many. Jimmy had returned for the same reason I had. Strangely, the fact that Jimmy wanted to visit a school, a teacher, failed to strike me as being out of character. Even though most people had always considered him a troublemaker, the trouble he made was outside of class, except when a teacher tried to impose some arbitrary authority on him; I had never heard of him disrupting classrooms or for that matter getting terrible grades. Miss Toole was busy, so we waited in the corridor. For the briefest of moments I wondered if he would be going to Classical, but dismissed that idea as crazy, and neither of us asked the other about school. We exchanged hellos, probably a handshake, and maybe a joke, and when we did visit with Miss Toole she paid each of us equal attention. To my shame, I remember thinking I should have gotten more.

He wasn't at Classical. But there my friends were not East Siders who had come with me from Bishop, but the kids from Olneyville and Federal Hill, the tough-kid Italian parts of the city. Perhaps my respect for Jimmy was partly the reason. Yet these friendships never lasted too long. Yes, anyone in the city could go to Classical, but kids often folded under the academic pressure and returned to junior high—Classical was ninth through twelfth grades, while the other public city high schools did not begin until tenth grade—or if they lasted one year, to Mount Pleasant or Hope or Central. My class had 450 students when we began ninth grade, and less than 200 graduated four years later. None of my friends were black anyway. Classical had four blacks out of 1,200 students. We did see blacks daily; Central High School and Classical shared the same gym. Central, although technically a comprehensive high school, was overwhelmingly black and sent almost no graduates to college, except for those who went on athletic scholarships (I well recall Bobby Thompson, who ran past me—at least he didn't run over me—for a fifty-seven-yard touchdown on his way to the NFL, and Marvin Barnes, who became an NBA All-Star); Central kids tried to intimidate us, especially the East Siders, with considerable success. Classical, especially East Siders, joked about the intelligence, or lack thereof, at Central. I did not.

Oh, I was a snob. In some ways maybe I still am, although my snobbery has always been based on intellect, not status. Brown was the only college I applied to. Harvard did not then attract me; since then I wish it had, but only because I am an elitist. I sneer when Rhode Island state legislators whine that Brown's medical program rejected every applicant from Providence College and the University of Rhode Island. What do you expect from PC and URI? I ask. But I do not sneer at those who did not go to school at all. I never felt anything but respect for Jimmy. I learned something from him, about invincibility when you don't give a damn. As Milton wrote, *So farewell hope, and with hope, farewell fear.* I envied Jimmy this invincibility more than I had envied his lunchtime freedom.

But there was far more to him than I am suggesting here and nothing is quite so simple as it seems. Trite as that sentiment may be, I don't think

I quite learned the truth of it until my last meeting with him. It was a chance encounter, on the East Side.

I was in college then, walking along Thayer Street. Jimmy was driving a truck—I think a garbage truck; it was filled with junk anyway—down Lloyd Avenue, and he stopped at the corner. He recognized me first. I heard my name called and looked up into a black face. He was happy to see me—so happy he was grinning.

I did not recognize him initially and, embarrassed, he started to tell me who he was. But before he did thankfully everything clicked in my head and I cut him off with a return grin.

We said "Hey," and I climbed onto the running board and stuck out my hand. For the only time ever that I knew him, Jimmy was suddenly uncertain. He was wearing heavy work gloves and he took off the right one, then, glancing hesitantly at his own hand, rubbed it against his shirt. "I don't want to get your hand dirty," he said. We shook, but he quickly thrust his hand back into the glove.

We talked briefly about Miss Toole and John Howland. "So what are you doing now?" I finally asked.

He spread his arms to take in the truck. "Working."

"Yeah. That makes sense. I bet you drive a truck." We laughed.

"How about you?"

I shrugged and sort of waved my arms to encompass the surroundings. We were in the center of the Brown University community.

"I go to Brown."

His eyes hungrily followed my gesture. A car honked. A fragment of the Jimmy I remembered leaned out of the window and told the driver to shut up. Then he turned back to me. "Brown, huh?" His eyes still held that hungry look. "I figured you for something like that."

That made sense too.

He pulled onto Thayer Street while I rode the running board.

I offered, "How about a beer?" We were in front of the College Hill Bookstore. Looking straight ahead, he refused. "Come on," I pleaded.

"I'm working," he said doggedly.

We crossed Angell Street and waited for the light at Waterman, surrounded by Brown buildings and Brown students. I asked once more, desperately suggesting Manny's, a bar where he would be comfortable and I would not.

"I'm working!" His voice was sharp. It carried within it both an obvious longing, even a jealousy for what I had, and a contempt for my failure to understand what the world was like.

A few seconds of silence, then, speaking now with an apologetic tone, he offered to drop me wherever I wanted. I was going to the library, the one named after Rockefeller. I told him right here was fine. Thanks a lot, hey, see you around. I didn't want him to take me to the Rockefeller Library. I asked him to meet me later. When would he get off work? He'd call me, he said. He swore he would.

Two months before I was graduated, still wrapped snugly in the warmth of my student deferment, Jimmy was killed in Vietnam.

WASHINGTON
The Players

Jimmy is why politics matter. To be blunt, not all people care about a just society, but that goal is something that moral people on both the left and right do seek. The struggle is over what defines a just society and the means of achieving it. Politics is where that struggle is fought.

As I said before, I began my first book intending to use Jim Wright's first term as Speaker of the House as a way to examine that struggle and explore how power is exercised in Washington, and both Wright and his most bitter of enemies Newt Gingrich cooperated with me.

Theirs was a classic confrontation. Wright was the last American political leader to take power whose values were forged in the Depression. He pursued his goals through the inside game, using parliamentary procedure to move legislation, and using his role as Speaker to influence even the country's foreign policies.

Gingrich was the first American political leader to rise to power entirely through his ability to manipulate the outside game, the media. Others before him had achieved some prominence and power as individuals by using the media, but as Gingrich rose he ultimately brought with him the whole Republican Party, winning control of the House for the first time in forty years. He nationalized the congressional races, at least temporarily turning on its head conventional wisdom and Tip O'Neill's maxim "All politics is local." For someone who was not even a presidential candidate to do this was utterly unheard of.

The media itself was and is a player as well. This is hardly new. Five hundred years ago Cardinal Thomas Wolsey said, "We must destroy the press, or the press will destroy us."

In the United States, journalists routinely remind us that the Founding Fathers wrote protection of the press into the Constitution. Speaking truth to power does matter, does protect freedom. *Thomas Jefferson even said,* "Were it left to me to decide whether we should have a government without newspapers, or newspapers without a government, I should not hesitate for a moment to prefer the latter."

Yet the reverence for a free press hardly means that the media is without flaws. Jefferson uttered the above comment before becoming president. His ideas, shall we say, evolved. As president he complained, "Nothing can now be believed which is seen in a newspaper. Truth itself becomes suspicious by being put into that polluted vehicle." And, "The man who never looks into a newspaper is better informed than he who reads them; inasmuch as he who knows nothing is nearer to truth than he whose mind is filled with falsehood and errors."

The media, Gingrich, and Wright are all players in this story, but it extends well beyond them, and beyond any simple narrative. This is the story of the death of one kind of politics, and the emergence of another.

In policy it marks the end of the New Deal, probably forever, for even if the passions that underlay the coalition constructed by Franklin Roosevelt return to American politics, the methods for translating those passions into policy will not return. The country has changed, and so has the country's faith in government.

But it also is the story of the end of a way of doing politics. The old way was not a bad way; in it political opponents respected each other, credited each other with good will, frequently worked together, and believed that compromise represented a positive good, not simply failure to achieve total victory. Typical of that old way, the harshest words spoken by former Speaker John McCormack were that he held his opponent in "minimal high regard." It was the way of insiders, but of insiders who were not corrupt, insiders who believed in what they were doing.

The new way increased the harshness, bitterness, destructiveness, and personal attacks in politics. It has turned the Congress into a place of extreme partisanship. The need to raise enormous sums of money has contributed to the rise of the new way. So have techniques of using the media. They have made the floor of the Congress, where legislation used to be worked out, less and less meaningful. But the change in how individuals play politics has contributed more. And politics is no spectator sport.

So the story of Wright and Gingrich and the media marks a divide, an end and a beginning.

THE MAKING OF A
POLITICIAN I

A t first Jim Wright seemed unimposing physically. Of average height, by the time he became Speaker his young man's leanness had given way to a soft and overlarge stomach. His only obvious physical features were his eyebrows—bushy and slanted upward, they gave him an almost Satanic cast—and even the eyebrows seemed relatively subdued now that he had aged and his flaming red hair had gone gray. Yet that first impression deceived. If he covered his mouth and inhaled deeply to yawn, his rib-cage would lift to reveal a barrel chest banded by muscle. And his presence...grew. In conversation he might suddenly focus intently, alert to every nuance of wording and facial expression and body language, his concentration so intense it was tactile, like fingers crawling on the skin, which could disconcert and intimidate. If he entered a room no magnetism drew people instantly to him, but gradually he would dominate more and more and more space, and more and more people would unconsciously give way to him.

He was highly intelligent and highly creative. There are really two kinds of brilliance: the vertical and horizontal. Those with the vertical kind dive deep into, penetrate, and analyze a single thing, gleaning from it truth and meaning that others could not. Those with a horizontal intelligence absorb information across a broad spectrum; they assimilate and weave together seemingly unconnected bits of data and as a result they can make what seems a creative leap. Wright had the latter kind: his was a listening, watching, waiting intelligence. When he acted he also prepared himself meticulously, and attended to details himself. Before he became Speaker, colleagues and reporters often confused his attention to detail with caution. But Wright was not cautious. He did not weigh and calculate the risk before choosing to act; on the contrary, often he would decide to take risks, dangerous risks, based on a private passion. He calculated and manipulated, as do all those whose goals can be achieved only through the compliance of others, but his calculations showed themselves when he executed his decision. They were not part of his decision-making process.

There were layers to Wright, and folds within layers. He had three passions really—a loner's desire to be liked, a missionary's desire to do good, and an achiever's raw ambition to leave a mark—and those three passions conflicted with each other, intertwined and wound about each other in a manner as complex as an Escher drawing. They simultaneously drove him and pulled him in different directions. Little showed on the surface, but under the surface the different currents could make the weave of his passions as twisted as a wound-up rubber band. The stresses on him sometimes could explode without warning. His voice, rich, soothing, not exactly deep but timbrous and resonant, was an orator's voice, but it hinted of something deep and dangerous.

The cemetery of Weatherford, Texas, seems less a graveyard than part of the bleached prairie that begins here and extends north and west for hundreds of miles, a hot, rolling land that bred generations who feared God, loved their country, and hated the banks. Jim Wright's parents are buried in this cemetery. Sitting in a car a few yards from their graves, he talked softly about them for a moment, saying, "They were very great people. My father had a wonderful flair. I'll never match it. . . . I was very fortunate to have had people who believed in me and taught me to believe in myself, told me I could do anything I wanted to, if I was willing to pay the price. . . . Mother was a patrician and Dad was an egalitarian. I suppose I inclined toward Dad's view, though I always cherished mother's belief in us and her insistence we were something special." He fell silent for a moment, then added, "I always thought I had to work twice as hard as anyone else to get anywhere."

His father had a reckless kind of charm which along with his courage could take him down dangerous paths. He used the second paycheck he ever got in his life to buy a newspaper advertisement attacking the Ku Klux Klan—this in a small Texas town at a time when the Klan was electing the mayors of Portland, Oregon, and Portland, Maine, controlling states like Indiana and Colorado, and sweeping across the south. More dangerous was the fact that he was a dreamer, a salesman who sold what he called "intangibles." "Any fool," he would say, "can sell a shoe, but ideas—it takes an artist to sell an idea."

His formal education ended in the fourth grade but he loved learning and read voraciously in literature, poetry, and history—his son would call him the best educated person he had ever known. A hero in World War I, he rose to captain despite his lack of formal schooling, was briefly a professional boxer, then sold oil leases, fund-raising gimmicks for charities, memberships in the U.S. Chamber of Commerce, and a dozen other things. Nothing took, though, and the family moved constantly. By the time young Jim got to high school, he had attended nine different schools in nine different towns. Small towns, cliquish towns. It was lonely for a new boy trying to find friends, more lonely than the loneliness of the prairie itself. Other boys had friends; young Jim had to work to make them. He smiled and learned quickly to give people what they liked, which was someone like themselves.

He began to hide himself a little. Instead of building a wall between himself and others, he constructed a sort-of two-way mirror that allowed him to see out while others saw their own reflection. From behind this screen, he measured how he should adjust to fit in. His outsider status had not embittered him; it had only made him wish to belong. "I did whatever Dad wanted me to do, whatever Coach wanted me to do," Wright said. "I wasn't a rebellious person. I wanted to be part of the team." There was a kind of deceit about it but he wasn't trying to deceive anyone, only please them, only win their approval. School came easy to him and he skipped grades, two full years by high school. Younger than his classmates, he lied about his age. What with all the moving, he could get away with it. His first ambition was to be a football coach because, in town after town where they lived, the coach was "the most admired man in the community."

His father taught him to box; that helped win respect. He was good, won tournaments, yet he wanted acceptance more than victory. In one boxing match against a boy he wanted as a friend, he dominated easily, then stopped hitting hard. He won, but his father berated him for letting up. Later young Jim overheard his parents arguing about it, heard his mother say, "Jim would rather have a friend than a victim."

His mother adored him. When he was ten or eleven, his mother started bringing him into the living room when adults visited, and he talked with them and charmed them and had things to say. "His mother thought he was the only perfect man," his first wife Mary Ethelyn "Mab" Lemmons said.

All the children, but Jim most of all, were taught ambition. The father, the nomad who moved from town to town carrying his own roots with him, filled the house with great expectations and taught his children to achieve, to make a mark, to imprint themselves on the world. His parents also taught their children to be concerned about and sensitive to what others thought. Their reputation, their good name, was the most important thing they had. Yet at the same time, carrying gossip was foul, evil. If one of the children repeated gossip, father or mother would say, "How do you know? Are you sure? Did you see it happen? You can't be besmirching people's names."

That did not mean blind conformity. Honor, being one's own person, and achievement, standing out, mattered more. The message took. There were three children. Jim was the oldest, then Mary, then Betty Lee. Betty Lee Wright became a college professor, wrote several textbooks, and designed part of the curriculum taught in Texas high schools. "She didn't do that because of any love of scholarship," says the middle child Mary Wright Connell. "She did it because a doctorate was as far as you could go. It was competitiveness."

Mary Connell had other dreams. She started writing poetry as a child and well into her fifties believed her life would be a failure if she did not win the Nobel Prize for literature. She published several books of poetry, and Graham Greene wrote a preface to one of her books saying he had discovered a wonderful new American poet. But the achievement and recognition she sought eluded her. With a touch of bitterness she once wrote,

> The child whose mother lets him yearn,
> for excellence, celebrity,
> or love, is done a dirty turn.
> Why cannot each: contented be
> with mannered love? accept advice?
> and hope next summer turns out nice?

Young Jim had ambition enough, too. Impatient, he respected no limits. But seeking acceptance, wanting to belong, he channeled his energy and disrespect for limits into achievement instead of rebellion. "I always wanted to do things *before*," he said. "I wanted to be the youngest to do this, the first to do that." Though he had skipped grades, he was easily an academic star. Though he was two full years younger than his schoolmates and smaller, he could whip them. He made his own rules. At thirteen, too young to enter a boxing tournament, he lied about his age and entered—and won the tournament. He dropped out of the University of Texas immediately after Pearl Harbor and volunteered. In the Army Air Corps, impatient to get into action, he picked up a phone, impersonated a senior officer, and ordered clerks to process his papers; he spent the war in the Pacific as a navigator on bombers. He was the only perfect man. Rules didn't apply to him.

At fifteen, he was addressing rallies for gubernatorial candidate Ernest Thompson, who had served in World War I with his father. Jim felt power over those crowds, felt his words wash over the crowd and return to him in waves of laughter, or anger, or warmth—whatever effect he sought. The crowd loved him, this precocious boy, loved him. The power and the crowd's embrace intoxicated him. "It's heady wine," Wright said. "You never get used to it."

His political views owed much to his father and to the Depression. The political driving force in the household remained a belief in equality. Mary Connell recalled, "The only prejudice we had was against Baptists who believed you would go to hell if you drank, danced, smoked, or played cards." Religion did matter, but the children were taught a loving, tolerant, forgiving God. Jim followed his father to different churches every week. Once, when Jim was making fun of Holy Rollers who claimed to hear God's music, his father told him to turn on the radio, then turn it off. "Do you hear the music now, Jim?" he asked. "Do you think they stopped playing or you just can't hear it?"

Everyone had hard times in the early 1930s, the Wrights included. The family moved in with Jim's grandparents in Dallas, and day after day Wright would look out the window and see his grandfather trudge up the walk with stooped shoulders after not finding work. Later Wright wrote, "There is hardly a greater shock to the nervous system than a feeling of uselessness." Everywhere Wright looked was pain. No one could avoid politics. Wright recalled, "Roosevelt seemed to identify with the problems of the people I knew, the plain people, and so I loved him."

He had what he himself called a "messianic impulse," and his ambition found a goal, *politics*. Woodrow Wilson especially attracted him; he read everything about Wilson and everything by him. One speech Wilson had made in Pueblo, Colorado, shortly before collapsing resonated within Wright. In that speech Wilson predicted that if America did not join the League of Nations, the war fought to make the world safe for democracy, his father's war, would prove to have been in vain and another generation would fight again. As Wright read that, the Japanese were in Manchuria, Italian Fascists were in Ethiopia, the Nazis were moving into Czechoslovakia. The Senate's refusal to join the League seemed a personal betrayal of Wright's father and of himself. Making such decisions, Wright thought, "That was something worthy of your efforts."

If Wright's sister Mary dreamed of the Nobel Prize, Wright wanted to be president.

Jim Wright's political career began immediately after the war. By then the family had money; one of his father's ideas had finally worked.

His first political involvement found him defending free speech at the University of Texas, and he was an organizer of a group of young liberal Democrats whose agenda included a world police force, medical care for the elderly, anti-lynching laws, and an end to the poll tax. In 1946 he ran for the state legislature and won, becoming at twenty-three its youngest member. There he led a fight to tax big oil companies to pay for roads and schools and voted to let blacks attend the University of Texas Law School.

Wright was the youngest, the most driven, and possibly the most liberal member in the legislature; he was as invulnerable and certain as youth itself. Then came his 1948 reelection campaign. Two opponents faced him. One was Eugene Miller, a gambler who reportedly had run big-money card games. Miller called him a communist dupe and accused Wright of wanting "every uppity nigra with a high school diploma" to go to the University of Texas Law School. Then, three weeks before the election, someone shot Miller.

In the hospital, Miller told people that Wright had nothing to do with the shooting. But he said "commies" and maybe Wright's "henchmen" had shot him. After he died, rumors swept Parker County. *Was Wright a murderer?*

At first Wright did nothing, believing no one could credit such a charge. It was ridiculous; though the crime was never solved, Texas Rangers found evidence that Miller had been killed for welching on gambling debts. But that conclusion came after the election. Wright's remaining opponent announced that he had received a bomb threat if he didn't withdraw. *The communists were behind Wright.*

Wright suddenly made the first compromise of principle of his political life. He took out a last-minute ad saying he supported the southern way of life, he "despised communism," and, "I believe in the Southern tradition of segregation and have strongly resisted any and all efforts to destroy it."

He lost by thirty-eight votes. The loss stunned him, embittered him. All his life he had worked for acceptance and the respect of others; instead he had been rejected. Meanwhile, he had bought 25 percent of the family business from his father and they were succeeding; the money was pouring in. Friends tried to interest him in running for mayor of Weatherford. He declined, and to punctuate the decision took a train to Chicago on business; the filing deadline for the mayor's race would pass while he was away. The train ride was a strangely passive act for him. It removed him from where he could act. But it also gave him time to do nothing but think and, with the rhythm of the railroad, watch the country, watch the country, watch the country. Mile after mile on his way north he thought about the sales meeting he was going to. *Was that what he wanted to do with his life? Just make money?*

He got off the train, picked up a telephone, and called a friend. "Can you file my papers?" he asked. "I'm going to run."

At twenty-six he became the youngest mayor in Texas. He built a house and took out a mortgage but the mortgage weighed on him. He hated debt; to him it was "enslavement" and, like his father, he would owe no man. He paid it off in four years. Meanwhile, as mayor, he did things. Damn the law. He was the law. When the gas utility threatened to cut off service to poorer neighborhoods, he told them, fine, but they wouldn't be able to service the rest of the city either. When one milk distributor advertised misleadingly, he told the distributor he could not sell in Weatherford unless the ads were corrected. He had no legal authority for those things, but he did them. His proudest moment came when he bought a reservoir from the Texas & Pacific railroad, and assured a water supply for the city. He had become a builder who could make something grow, a doer. He became the youngest president ever of the association of Texas mayors.

In business, too, he prospered, but more than ever the two-way mirror glistened, more than ever he could see out but others could not see in. He was secretive. "He never let me know how much money he was making," his first wife Mab recalled, "that was part of his manipulation, having his finger on everything."

She was convinced he was making over $70,000 a year. That was an extraordinary amount of money in the early 1950s; by comparison, congressmen made $12,500. He wasn't thirty yet.

When Wright and she had started dating seriously he told her he planned to run for Congress in ten years. His high school yearbook predicted he would be in Congress in 1955.

At thirty-one, in 1954, he ran for the United States House of Representatives against Congressman Wingate Lucas, a conservative supported by Fort Worth newspaper owner Amon Carter. Labor backed Wright. Years earlier, just back from the war and full of his own future, Wright had introduced himself to Carter at a picnic. Carter had snubbed him cold. Wright remembered. The day before the election Wright ran a full-page ad in Carter's paper: "You have at last met a man, Mr. Carter, who is not afraid of you, who will not bow his knee to you, and come running like a simpering pup at your beck and call."

There was a self-righteousness in that language, and ego, but it struck a populist chord. Jim Wright romped to victory. He was thirty-one when he was elected, right on track with the promise he had made to Mab, on track with the prediction in his high school yearbook, on track to power.

In Congress he quickly learned the verities of politics, the slow relentless corrosive power of compromise, the exposure to the worst instincts of people as well as the best, the increasing strain of maintaining a public persona and a private self. The persona dominated.

Passions in the land forced the submergence of his own self and his own passions. In 1954 the Supreme Court outlawed segregation in Brown v. Board of Education. The decision was ripping the South apart. It could destroy a young southern congressman like snapping one's fingers. He said the Supreme Court had "erred in judgement." Soon after his election Wright faced a large audience in a small-town high school gym. He wanted to talk about schools and roads and waterworks and building the country when a woman hissed, "What are you gonna do about them niggers?" He ignored the question but she interrupted again. "*What are you gonna do about them niggers?*" Hesitating, inhaling deeply, he began to talk, about being born out there himself, he knew how she felt, but tolerance was a good Christian thing, and the Supreme Court had decided and the law was the law and they had elected him to uphold the law. That was the language liberals in the South used to protect themselves. Afterwards, driving home with his closest friend and aide Craig Raupe, he sighed, "I'm awful tired of people."

He showed courage in refusing to sign the "Southern Manifesto," which denounced the court decision, one of just five southerners in Congress to refuse, three of whom lost reelection. But he also said, "I feel that segregation could be ideally maintained without discrimination, that it is possible for facilities to be equal while being separate." He survived.

He hid himself, now more than ever. It was nothing new, really. After the war he had worked as a salesman briefly, and before each appointment used to tell himself, *I'm going to like this person, I wish him well, and he's going to like me.* It was a veil he wore, a smiling cordial front that reflected his control over himself; he kept himself private even from himself. Rarely did the veil lift, even with his wives. His second wife Betty, whom he married in 1972, said, "He talks about his childhood as if everything was always perfect but I wonder. His father was an alcoholic but he never talks about that. I learned that from his sisters, not from him."

He wore his smile constantly. "He is a controlled man," Mab said. "You do not know what he is thinking. I never knew if something upset him because his reaction was always to laugh."

There was something chilling in this element of the man. Yet if he was a mystery, if he hid himself sometimes from even himself, then behind the mirror, behind the relentless smile, there the equally relentless drive and the equally relentless passion burned.

On policy, he began to make a mark despite his junior status. He offered a plan to establish a sinking fund to pay off the national debt which attracted some press attention but nothing else. Other plans had greater luck. He went to see President Dwight Eisenhower to convince him to abandon a plan to pay for the interstate highway system with a bond issue, and instead support a pay-as-you-go gasoline tax. Eisenhower agreed and Wright's plan became law. He also did well by Fort Worth, which according to one study, had the highest per capita federal spending of any district in the nation. Inside the House he was winning respect; he was one of the members who knew substance and, even if a mystery personally, did not lie. That gave him influence over other votes. People would come to him and ask about things; he would tell them straight out what a bill would or wouldn't do and let them decide for themselves. They came to rely upon him.

After a failed attempt to replace Lyndon Johnson in the Senate—Wright finished third of seventy-one candidates, just missing a run-off most observers thought he would have won—he turned his ambition toward the House. He was also frustrated.

He was in his forties. His intensity still burned but to what end? His hobbies were all lonely, personal pursuits. Some required absolute concentration: flying, boxing—he trained into his fifties and once planned an exhibition match with then heavyweight champion Joe Frazier until Speaker John McCormack cancelled it, calling it undignifed. Other hobbies—writing (he wrote four books and his own speeches), painting, gardening—produced something. He explained, "I am alert to the inexorable movement of the hand on the clock, the pages on the calendar.... What do you have after two hours of golf? If I spend two hours in the garden I have something to show for it."

Wright no longer seemed quite so marvelous to Mab, and she resented that he seemed to be performing when he came home just as he did inside the House. "He has to be all things to all people," she said. "Even to me he wanted to appear as I thought he was. When it got to the point where I couldn't see him that way, that's where I think our marriage fell apart."

Then a lowly rung on the leadership ladder opened. Jack Brooks was giving up his job as one of four deputy whips, men who counted votes for the leadership and convinced members to vote for leadership positions. Did Wright want it? The leadership would prefer a Texan, and Brooks would help him get it. Brooks said, "I wasn't willing to take the time away from my family. Jim was."

In 1969 he and Mab began a two-year legal separation. She told him to leave. A secretary named Betty Hay had started working for him in 1965. They were the same age and he started seeing her. Betty had had a hard life. Growing up poor in St. Louis, as a teenager she had danced in shows while her mother looked for work. She was tough, independent, would not take guff from anybody, had herself been a loner, had a brief failed marriage of her own, considered herself a failure. They were drawn to each other. At first, Wright did not want to marry again. But in 1972 his divorce became final. Later that year he and Betty married. Speaking of that time, Betty later told the *Washington Post*, "Men feel like a failure, too."

It was a telling remark. At their age, they would not have children. All they would have was his career, his success, his fulfilment. But what was his career?

On his fiftieth birthday he reviewed his life in his journal. For the first time he admitted, formally, that he never would be president. He tried to reconcile himself to that failure, but his words rang with hollow and wintry tones. Soon, inevitably, he would become chairman of the Public Works Committee, but that accomplishment seemed to mock him, mock everything he had once dreamed of being and doing.

That career was . . . not what he had dreamed of.

As he faced more frustration, he wrote an "affirmation" which he carried in his pocket and pondered daily until it became "ingrained." In it he inadvertently described his rigid self-control, and a volcano of ambition and insecurity rumbling beneath that self-control. It began: "This is the day the Lord has made; I shall be glad and rejoice in it. . . . I shall surely not let others upset me, nor rob me of my serenity. No person can take from me my inner peace, for I shall quietly, calmly, gently, pleasantly hold onto it—for it is mine, a gift of God, and with it I can do anything. . . . I shall be open to new things, new thoughts, new truths that I can learn from other people. . . . I have performed well in the past, and I fully expect success in the future. . . . I deserve to have happiness, career success, and economic security. . . . The Lord wants me to have them. . . . Because I like and respect myself, I am not adversely affected by the attitudes of others. If they think they do not like me, it is because they do not know me."

But when the position of majority leader opened in 1976, he took one final shot at power, jumping into the race as the longest shot of the four candidates running. He won by a single vote. Suddenly all that he had abandoned hope of achieving seemed once again possible.

He spent ten years as majority leader under Speaker Tip O'Neill, during which Wright's view of the House crystalized. "The House is the institution closest to the people," he said. "Every member who ever served in it was elected. That cannot be said of the presidency or the Senate. The House is the raw essence of the nation."

That interpretation gave the House authority. And the speaker was the leader of the House. It allowed him to believe that his authority was derived from the nation itself. Like the president.

And who was Wright now, as he became Speaker of the House? Analyzing his own style he said, "It's like simultaneously playing chess and ping-pong. A lot of what I do isn't calculated in some arcane sense, but a lot of what I say to a member is calculated in ways in which I have only a vague sense myself. I don't think consciously of this strategy or that tactic. Things are too fluid for that. I have goals in mind and pursue those goals."

Calculation had become so ingrained in him as to no longer be conscious. That was hardly unique to Wright. He often quoted the saying of Lincoln, the great lonely and stoic figure among presidents, that the best way to destroy an enemy was to make him a friend. But Wright, except when his passion exploded to the surface, showed his real self rarely even by Washington standards.

Nor did he reveal himself to colleagues, even over the years. "Who are his friends?" Dan Rostenkowski, the Illinois Democrat who chaired the most powerful committee in the Congress, Ways and Means, asked. "Nobody knows. Who's he go out to dinner with? Nobody knows. Everybody knows who Tip's friends were. Everyone knows who I go out to dinner with." "When you go on trips," said another congressman, "you spend six, seven days with your colleagues, you get to know them, talk about your family, your kids. Wright never talks about his kids. In fact, I don't even know if he has kids." Former Texas Congressman Bob Eckhardt, who first met Wright in 1946, forty years later said, "I don't know if he has kids either." (He has four.) Always a loner, never a natural politician, he worked to be charming. His closest friend Craig Raupe noted, "Jim can go to a social event and charm people but that's work for him, that's hard work. . . . If you've had two or three moments of real intimacy with him, that's a lot." Wright described himself in his private journal as "secretive."

He had a sense that rules did not apply to him. The corruptive force of power did not give him that sense. But it was there. It showed itself in an occasional wild flash in his eyes, and it came from a faith that he could succeed where others failed. It made him willing to put everything he had on the line. Thirty-two years in the House had taught him about boundaries, about the limits of power, but that sense made him willing to try to create new boundaries. There was an innocence, if not naivete, in that, too.

A very thin line divides innocence and arrogance. A small child has both. The child believes the world centers on itself and refuses to recognize limits on what he or she expects and demands. Later, as the child matures, innocence and arrogance become distinguishable.

There are several kinds of innocence. One involves experience—being unsullied. And yet innocence can remain despite any sullying experience. One is innocent to the extent one ignores experience and exposes oneself, risks oneself, to the present and future. Most people, usually because of pain and past failure, lose this kind of innocence and accept the limits of the world.

Arrogance assumes that one can do almost anything, either because one can get away with it, or because—and in this way arrogance approaches a kind of innocence—one believes that whatever one does must be all right. Part of the corruption of idealism, the corruption of power, stems from the blurring of innocence and arrogance, and the confusion of expectation and demand.

Wright, for all his ability to manipulate, for all his experience in thirty-two years in Congress, retained a certain innocence. Underneath the surface, not showing, were rumblings, both within himself and within the House. Wright had already extended his reach far enough to rub up against limits members expected him to respect. What would happen if he bunched his fist and tried to punch a hole in those limits? No one knew. But the first rumblings were there.

Republican Newt Gingrich recognized the rumblings and observed, "He creates himself when he acts."

And for all Wright's relentless courtesy, a courtesy which could border on obsequy—his bending over to pick up a pencil someone else had dropped; his pouring coffee for others—there was something else about him, too. A tension ran through him and others sensed it. That smile of his, that omnipresent, impossible-to-read killer smile unnerved people. He seemed a dangerous man, a man not to be trifled with, a man to be handled gently. Several times Wright had almost got into fistfights on the floor. GOP Congressman and now Vice President Dick Cheney said, "You get the sense you wouldn't want to cross him."

Still before Wright's ascension to Speaker, one Democratic colleague remarked, "I think Wright's strength is at the level of getting new rugs put in members' offices. Maybe he can translate that into legislative victories."

That statement signified how little even Wright's colleagues knew of him, or understood him, or expected of him. His colleagues would soon learn about him, about a powerful man, a man they could not read.

When the 100th Congress of the United States convened on January 6, 1987, Jim Wright became Speaker of the House of Representatives, the most powerful position in the Congress. Wright had waited thirty-two long years for power. He intended to use it for more than putting rugs in members' offices.

THE MAKING OF A
POLITICAN II

In April 1987, only weeks into the speakership of Jim Wright, Newt
Gingrich reached a decision. Wright had already masterminded the
passage of major legislation and the budget as well as the override
of two Reagan vetoes; he was forcing changes on taxes, moving an om-
nibus trade bill forward, and spreading his influence into every area of
policy from welfare to foreign affairs.

Gingrich observed, "As far as operational effectiveness inside the
House, you'd have to give Wright an A-plus. We're completely disorga-
nized as a result. He's just tougher. Trent"—Trent Lott, then House
GOP whip—"complains about how tough his people are. [Dave] Bonior
on Rules. [Tony] Coelho's whip operation. Our leadership has no idea
how to handle Wright." And he worried, "If Wright ever consolidates his
power, he will be a very, very formidable man. We have to take him on
early to prevent that."

If the House Republican leadership had no idea how to handle Wright,
Gingrich had an idea how to handle him.

At the time, Gingrich was little more than a junior back-bencher
known for extreme partisanship and the ability to generate media attention. Elected in 1978, by the usual standards of performance measure-
ment for a representative—legislation passed or influenced, federal dollars
collected for his district—he had accomplished almost nothing. Indeed,
there were 435 congressional districts in America, and 425 of them got
more federal dollars than his; this was remarkable indeed, considering
his district included one of the largest airports in the country.

But Gingrich measured himself by a different standard. In his office
he did not work at a conventional desk, but used a podium that he stood
at, pacing constantly back and forth as he thought or talked. He was

forty-four years old, an age by which most people know whether their lives will fulfill or betray their ambitions. His hair was gray, prematurely so, his belly soft in the way of those who had never done athletic things as opposed to those whose youthful leanness has been overtaken by age. Before entering Congress he had been a professor of modern European history, and he still had his professorial air, engaging in sharp intellectual debate with peers and lecturing others. At the 1984 Republican Convention he had declared, "This is my campus. . . . I'm conducting seminars."

The seminars dealt with how to achieve power, for he focused not on legislation but on power itself. He approached the question in the abstract, as if it were purely theoretical, requiring theoretical solutions. The excitement of the analysis attracted him; it was immensely more challenging and had many more levels than a chess game.

There was a coldness about him, the coldness of raw intellect, of absolute zero, and little passion. In 1980 his first wife lay in the hospital recovering from cancer surgery when he walked in, said he planned to divorce her, and pulled out a yellow legal pad filled with details of a settlement. She was still woozy from the surgery. He wanted her to sign it. Lee Howell, once close enough to Gingrich to ask him to be his best man, told *Mother Jones* writer David Osborne, "[Newt] handled the divorce like he did any other political decision: You've got to be tough in this business, you've got to be hard. Once you make the decision you've got to act on it. Cut your losses and move on."

Gingrich described himself as "an Army brat," and, like Wright, had moved from place to place as a boy. But where Wright worked hard to make friends everywhere, Gingrich reacted differently to the rootlessness, exploring the reaches of his own mind. When he was fifteen he visited Verdun, one of the bloodiest battles of World War I, and was terrified and haunted by one monument which contains the remains of 130,000 French and German troops, bones upon bones, a concrete manifestation of what power could do. Within months he wrote a 180-page analysis of world power and announced he would become a Republican congressman. Once in Congress he talked of his "inner strength that other politicians don't have" and "a calling."

The inner strength, the calling, the intellectualism made him ruthless, and ruthless in the coldest way. One House Republican said, "He has what the contras would call 'soft hands'—he would pull strings while others crawled through the jungle. Another House Republican noted, "Let's just say I wouldn't want to get in Newt's way."

Yet to those who enjoyed discussing ideas, Gingrich was a pleasure to be around. He did not bluff, did not pretend to know something he did not; when someone mentioned existentialism, for example, Gingrich said he didn't fully understand it and therefore couldn't contribute anything to the conversation.

Once he had been moderate: Eisenhower was one of his heroes, and he had worked in Nelson Rockefeller's presidential campaign against Goldwater. But that was a long time ago. After the collapse of House GOP dreams of taking control of the House in 1982, he became the prime mover behind the "Conservative Opportunity Society," which grew out of a debate over strategy of how to make the GOP the majority party in the House and the nation.

Ideologically, COSers scorned the old right wing of the party, the Wall Street pin-striped crowd. They were the New Right, committed Reaganites and populists who would link up with and help energize the Christian right. Reasoning that the GOP had tried cooperation in legislation with Democrats for years and gotten no where, the COS abandoned accommodation, felt no responsibility to govern or to help Democrats pass anything. The group began as a tiny minority, but by the time Wright became Speaker it included roughly 20 percent of House Republicans. Led by Gingrich, they pursued their agenda outside the Congress. Indeed, they used the Congress largely as a prop to frame issues for the media.

As part of this strategy, in 1984 Gingrich accused several Democrats by name of being "blind to communism," and threatened to "file charges" against ten of them—including Wright—for sending a letter to Nicaraguan President Daniel Ortega which addressed him as "Dear Commandante." Ortega was supported by the Soviet Union. (Wright wrote the letter after the Reagan administration asked him to try to influence Ortega, and the letter itself urged Ortega to hold free elections.) Gingrich had made the accusation from the floor of the House, when the House was operating under "special orders," which meant no legislative business could be conducted but the proceedings were televised. When Gingrich made his attack, the only congressmen present in the vast chamber were two or three Republicans, and not a single Democrat, who wanted to address the TV audience. (The camera focused tightly on whoever was speaking so the audience could not see that the chamber was empty.)

The next day during a regular session on the House floor Speaker Tip O'Neill called Gingrich's comment "the lowest thing that I've ever seen in my thirty-two years in Congress," launching a bitter partisan exchange that was shown on all three network news shows. This taught Gingrich something. Soon after he pointed out to conservative activists that for months he had been giving "organized, systematic, researched one-hour lectures. Did CBS rush in . . . ? No. But the minute Tip O'Neill attacked me, he and I got ninety seconds on all three network news shows. The number-one fact about the news media is that they love fights. When you give them confrontations you get attention. When you get attention, you can educate."

So Gingrich began applying his lesson, attacking Democrats in ways that got media attention. His goal was to have the media quote him and others saying the same thing so often that what they said would be taken at face value. He wanted to create what he called "resonance," resonance *out there*, in the country. This could also influence the questions reporters asked, the stories they chose to cover. Two years before Wright became Speaker, Gingrich commented, "We are engaged in reshaping a whole nation through the news media." Gingrich, the former professor of modern European history who would soon be comparing Wright to Mussolini, was perhaps familiar with Mussolini's observation, "Another weapon I discovered early was the power of the printed word to sway souls to me. The newspaper was soon my gun."

The target of this gun would be Wright.

Gingrich's campaign began with an abstraction. In 1985, he sat eating lunch in the member's dining room, grabbed a napkin, and drew a triangle on it, labeling the sides of the triangle "reality," "personal lives," and "people's values," and explained, "All successful politicians have to be inside the triangle. Democrats grew outside of it with things like gay rights."

It was a capsule analysis of what matured into a driving theme of his in the future, an effort to define Democrats as permanently outside the triangle, outside the mainstream of American values and symbols—and thus define them out of existence.

Another Gingrich abstraction was a construct of "all human activities," which he arranged in a hierarchy: "Vision is at the top of that. What is your vision of what you're doing? Then once you have a vision, what is your strategy?... What are the projects that you've assigned to do that?... The bottom level after vision, strategies, and projects is tactics.... One of the major problems of the Republican Party is that we focus on tactics. The result is that the vision and strategy level of the left kills you."

Vision. Strategy. Projects. Tactics.

Gingrich's vision was the achievement of power.

It was power which had fascinated him ever since his visit to the World War I battlefield of Verdun. It was power about which he had written a 180-page study while still in high school. And nothing drove home the ramifications of power, and its ruthlessness, like the subject of modern European history which he had taught. Gingrich was pure analysis; he looked for weakness, for something to exploit, and when he found it he went after it coldly and methodically.

His strategies toward achieving power were twofold. First, he preached the creation of his "Conservative Opportunity Society." Its essence was the entrepreneur, and its devil was the "statist" government which had developed in the preceding half century. Stressing low taxes, Gingrich once called Bob Dole "the tax collector for the welfare state." In this, Gingrich borrowed from the anti-establishment, pro-little guy, libertarian streak that ran deep in American life.

But Gingrich was no inflexible ideologue. He talked of inner peace, but that peace came not from faith but from intellectual self-confidence, or perhaps from a faith in the correctness of his analysis.

As a result, his Conservative Opportunity Society was not well defined and lacked the emotional pull of Ronald Reagan's strong simple themes. Indeed, Gingrich blurred his ideological message by rejecting Reagan's statement that "government is the problem." Instead he sounded much like the new centrist breed of Democrat when he demanded an activist, aggressive government. He just did not want a big government. He explained, "We created airlines by subsidizing air mail. We created the microchip industry through the Pentagon. These were conscious strategies. There's a big difference between a big, bureaucratic government, neutrality, and privatization—" using the government to get the private sector to advance social goals.

His second strategy involved values. Gingrich understood that the religious right wing of the GOP was most interested in values—the anti-abortionists, the Moral Majority supporters—and intended to mobilize those groups as shock troops. But he also recognized these groups were threatening to many people and warned, "If we allow the fundamentalists to dictate party policy, we doom ourselves to being a permanent minority."

His projects were to destroy trust in the Democratic Party and in government itself. He did not plan on advancing his objectives legislatively. He intended to use the House floor and his position as a congressman to influence the media and, through it, the world outside Congress. It was a destructive, not constructive, force which he hoped to generate. He didn't invent such tactics. Joe McCarthy aside, former House GOP leader John Rhodes had first claimed that after ruling the House for, at the time he wrote his book *The Futile System*, almost twenty years the Democratic Party had itself become systematically corrupt.

Gingrich decided to adopt and expand that theme. "The Democrats have run the House for more than thirty years," he said. "They've gotten sloppy. The House is a corrupt institution, corrupt in the Lord Acton sense."

He would talk about systematic corruption in the House. And he became convinced that ethics could become a major issue. "The cover of *Time* deals with ethics," Gingrich said. "Tammy Faye and Jim Bakker [TV evangelists who were exposed as con artists and possibly sexual deviants], all these things are ethical issues." Ethics was also important because of "the sleaze factor"—a reference to all the Reagan administration officials who had ethics problems, or even gone to prison, and to the expectation the issue could be important in the next presidential election. Various senior administration officials were convicted of criminal wrong-doing, including White House aide and Reagan confidant Michael Deaver, White House political director Lyn Nofziger (his conviction was later overturned), and Deputy Defense Secretary Paul Thayer, while Labor Secretary Raymond Donovan had been tried and acquitted. There were dozens of others. Indeed, GOP assistant attorney general William Weld, later governor of Massachusetts, resigned saying said that Attorney General Edwin Meese should have been indicted; Meese had inappropriately helped and had accepted favors from people convicted of fraud and bribery.

Gingrich believed he could do more than simply dispel this sleaze factor. He intended to attack and attack and put Democrats on the defensive. But discussing corruption in the Lord Acton sense was far too abstract to make the front pages. He needed something concrete. He intended to personalize his charges in the body of Jim Wright.

In the spring of 1987, he decided to demand, at some future time, an investigation of Wright. He assigned an aide full-time to dig up anything negative on him she could find, going back to his first entry into public life. But he would pace himself. Once before he had tried to move something prematurely and failed. It taught him a lesson: "I got ahead of myself. I was proposing a solution before the public understood there was a problem."

He would not make that mistake again. He would try to build public perception of questionable behavior, and then strike.

His tactic was to create stories. In advance, while his aide looked for dirt on Wright, he tried to generate "resonance" in the media. On July 21, 1987, he wrote Fred Wertheimer, president of Common Cause, who had credibility with the press which Gingrich himself lacked. Gingrich's letter included long, detailed accusations against several Democrats— but no Republicans—including Wright and House whip Tony Coelho. The accusations had meat. Gingrich urged Wertheimer to demand action on these charges from the House Ethics Committee. Eight days later Wertheimer did what Gingrich asked, writing the Ethics Committee—repeating the details and some of the language in Gingrich's letter—and demanding action against the members Gingrich had named except for Wright and Coelho. Wertheimer also charged that the committee "has abdicated its responsibility to vigorously and effectively enforce the ethics rules and standards that apply to members of the House of Representatives."

Wertheimer gave his letter to the press; his attack got media attention. Gingrich also staged a "special order," televised over C-SPAN, on the same subject attacking the various members carefully, within the restrictive framework of House rules. It created more resonance. Gingrich was more than satisfied. He hadn't expected Wertheimer and Common Cause to call for an investigation of Wright—not yet anyway. That would take time, but Gingrich had time. The reward for his patience might be power.

One political ally sent him a memo saying the ethics issue "strikes a rich vein that can be mined for Party advantage in regaining congressional numbers and influence." And a second political adviser asked in a memo, *"What is your strategy for the ethics issue over the long-term?* [italics his] i.e., how often should [Pennsylvania Republican Congressman Robert] Walker offer his ethics resolution? What Democratic members should have FEC and ethics filings scrutinized? Is there a better way than filing a complaint" with the Ethics Committee?

Gingrich sent a copy of this memo to Joseph Gaylord, another ally who ran the GOP House campaign committee, the organization dedicated to electing Republican congressmen.

And Gingrich himself began to prepare his attack on Wright.

His aide had dug up some old critical newspaper stories. When Wright became majority leader he held a fund-raiser and transferred the money to his personal use; he had not hidden the fact and claimed he was only repaying himself for money he had spent on his Senate campaign fifteen years earlier. What Wright did was legal at the time, but soon became illegal. He had also lobbied Egyptian President Anwar Sadat on behalf of a Texas oilman with whom he had invested. There were some other small things and one big thing: Wright was largely blamed for delaying passage of legislation regulating the savings and loan industry at the request of many S&L executives who had given big money to the Democratic Party and opposed the bill. The entire industry was suffering a melt-down that would ultimately cost taxpayers tens of billions of dollars. Stories of corruption within the industry were rife. These things smelled bad. Every critical clipping went into a file, and Gingrich started giving these clippings to reporters. That meant that even stories written about Wright's policy successes would raise some question about his ethical judgement.

He understood that if the press believed that Wright was corrupt, it would go after him: "The media values its liberal bias less than it values honesty in government." He was right. The Washington bureau chief of one of the world's most powerful newspapers confirmed, "If I ever become convinced that someone in public office is corrupt, I will never, ever give him a break, on anything."

Gingrich recognized that if he could sell reporters the idea that Wright had engaged in questionable past dealings while simultaneously charging systemic corruption—his theme of a corrupt House, corrupted by power, by thirty-two years of Democratic rule—he might really have something. He and several COS colleagues began working on a book to be called *A House of Ill Repute*. Democrats ran Congress. Wright ran the Democrats. At the least, any damage inflicted on either had to help House Republicans and keep Wright from consolidating his power.

Then Gingrich became more aggressive, urging editors and writers across the country to investigate Wright. He tried unsuccessfully for grandslam home-runs—getting Ted Koppel's *Nightline* show and *Sixty Minutes* to raise the issue of corruption in the House, and specifically of Jim Wright. When those efforts failed, he began in methodical fashion to build resonance, to make a record of charges in the print media in cities all over the country, like a ball-player working his way up through the minors.

Whenever he visited a city—and as the leading intellectual light of the New Right he traveled often to make speeches and attend colleagues' fund-raisers—he would try to talk to local political reporters, local investigative reporters, local editorial writers, and plant seeds with them.

He also began offering reporters a powerful attributed quote. Few people in Washington publicly attack anyone, much less the Speaker of the House. In July 1987, he told a reporter for the first time, "Wright's the least ethical Speaker of the twentieth century."

That quote got attention and guaranteed that any reporter writing about Wright would talk to Gingrich, hoping to get an inflammatory comment. A personal attack added vitality to any story. Gingrich was more than happy to oblige and would repeat it and repeat it. It helped create a sense of smoke.

Now, in the summer of 1987 after another policy triumph by Wright, Gingrich was sitting on a couch in his office explaining his goal: to use media pressure to force a House Ethics Committee investigation of Wright. If the investigation started, he knew the press attention would require an independent counsel. Although he knew of nothing Wright had done wrong Gingrich said, "What I really want is to get some people with subpoenas poking around. He's from Texas. He's been in politics thirty years. There's got to be something.

"Look, I don't think Jim Wright's a Mafia don. . . . Wright's a useful keystone to a much bigger structure. I'll just keep pounding and pounding on his ethics. There comes a point where it comes together and the media takes off on it, or it dies."

For a moment Gingrich, his jacket off, sipping a scotch, switched subjects, and marveled at Wright's performance as Speaker. Gingrich raised his glass, stared into it for a moment, and said, "If Wright survives this ethical thing, he may become the greatest Speaker since Henry Clay."

THE MEDIA

The press is always this great *thing* out there in politics. Two centuries ago Edmund Burke observed, "There are three estates in parliament, but in the reporters' gallery yonder, there sits a fourth estate more important by far than them all."

The fourth estate. Heavy, ponderous, powerful, and potentially dangerous, its relationship with those in power is a complex one: simultaneously symbiotic, parasitic, and adversarial, with subject and object constantly reversing roles. Depending on mood and individuals, the media can be as cold and relentless as a glacier carving out a gorge, or as intimate as college roommates exchanging stories about their sexual experiences, or as vicious as dogs ripping at one small piece of exposed flesh.

In the narrowest, inside-the-Beltway sense, the press was used to communicate between factions of policy-makers inside Washington. This is a world of nuance and interpretation. In this role, the three most important newspapers, the *Washington Post, New York Times,* and *Wall Street Journal,* serve almost as a messenger service between those who affect what government actually *does*—the laws it writes, the regulations it enforces, the edicts it passes down. Policy-makers use the three dailies to stake out positions, declare themselves, feel out others for responses and force them to define their positions. Television rarely gets into this part of the game. The daily struggle over the details of governing, and subtlety, escape it. The print media allows such analysis. One even gets print on one's fingers; one has to wash it off. Print has feel, color, smell. It is tangible, there, a thing to mark up, copy, pass around and read and reread and file and look up a year later and think about and consider and grow angry over or happy over. Any story, or for that matter an unattributed quote, in any of the three main papers is attended to and analyzed by others concerned with a particular issue.

Newt Gingrich ignored that narrow function of the press as he ignored policy. His interest lay in the power the press has to set the agenda and to define its own reality. His interest lay in the power of perception, and the press controls that particular power. It always has.

There are two chief paradoxes in the relationship between journalists and the powerful:

First, despite the media's generally adversarial tone and its aggressiveness—and this is nothing new—it is almost entirely reactive in choosing what stories to cover. This reactiveness amounts almost to passivity, and leaves the media open to manipulation and exploitation. The press is both subject and object; it affects issues and people it covers, and yet can be manipulated in its selection of stories and the way it covers them.

Second, as in many competitive professions the very competitiveness of the media yields a sameness. Success breeds imitation. Also, its members have large egos and large insecurities, and want simultaneously to stand out from the pack and to be confirmed by it.

The most obvious aspect of the relationship between journalists and those they cover is the adversarial tone reporters take. The press sees itself as the judge of politicians, the monitor of the state. This institutional sense of separateness, of sitting in judgement, is not simply an abstract concept; it shows itself tangibly each year at the president's state of the union speech. Out of simple courtesy everyone in the House chamber— members of both parties in House and Senate, judges of the Supreme Court, members of the diplomatic community, everyone in the galleries looking on—applauds the president when he is introduced. Except, that is, for one silent pocket, one dead hole of silence in the chamber; journalists in the press gallery, directly above and behind the dais, sit silently, making no motion of approval or disapproval. It is easy to see how a member of Congress might look up and sneer, *Objective? Ha! Obnoxious hypocrites is more like it.*

Yet for all its adversarial nature, the media's agenda is imposed upon it. Rarely do reporters actually generate stories. They react, they receive. The line between subject and object becomes blurred. Stories come from events: a floor vote, a press conference, a terrorist bombing, a leak. The Pentagon came under media attack over scandals of spending such ludicrous amounts as hundreds of dollars for a hammer after congressional committees either leaked or held public hearings following their investigations. No investigative journalist broke the story with digging; the press simply reported what either the Pentagon itself or congressional investigators disclosed.

Even when investigative reporters do expose new information, they rarely are true "enterprise" stories, i.e., stories generated entirely by a reporter. Most investigative pieces start with a leak, and leaks serve the purpose of the leaker; they represent an effort to manipulate the media.

Seymour Hersh of the *New York Times* won a Pulitzer Prize for breaking the story of My Lai, where American troops lined up several hundred Vietnamese civilians and machine-gunned them. He did so after Ron Ridenhour, a soldier, sent a 1,500-word letter to the *Times*, congressional committees, and the joint chiefs of staff detailing what happened, and including the names and rank of witnesses who would attest to it. In effect, Hersh won a Pulitzer for rewriting Ridenhour's letter and interviewing the witnesses Ridenhour identified for him—and Hersh admitted as much at Tulane University on a 1994 panel with Ridenhour and David Halberstam, who had covered Vietnam for the *Times* and called Ridenhour a "hero."

Charles Babcock, an investigative reporter for the *Washington Post*, did break stories about Reagan's Attorney General Ed Meese, and would break others about both Wright and Gingrich. Speaking of the Meese scandals, he said, "It was all public information. Nobody believed that. Even my own editors thought it was leaked to me." Even his own editors believed someone had handed him key bits of information.

In the first weeks of George Bush senior's administration, stories suddenly appeared about Secretary of State Jim Baker's ownership of several million dollars worth of Chemical Bank stock—and he had owned it while treasury secretary, while making decisions every day about Third World loans that greatly increased the stock's value. Yet Baker had listed his ownership on financial disclosure forms. No reporter bothered to review those forms for four years, until he became secretary of state, and, even then, the story was leaked to reporters by White House counsel Boyden Gray, who later admitted mentioning Baker to reporters. Gray had come under attack himself because for the eight years he had worked for Bush while Bush was vice president, Gray had continued to serve as chairman of the board of, and accepted hundreds of thousand dollars in salary from, a $250 million family company. Brooks Jackson, then a *Wall Street Journal* investigative reporter (now with CNN), said, "That's a black mark on all of us [journalists], that we didn't uncover that Baker stuff."

The media's generally adversarial tone masks its passivity, masks the fact that it has had its agenda imposed upon it. Former White House Press Secretary Larry Speakes expressed the tension between the manipulators and the manipulated when he told reporters, "Don't tell me how to manage the news and I won't tell you how to report it."

How the media reports stories is a function of other factors, of the interplay between reporters' and editors' sense of responsibility and fairness, their egos, and their publication's (or broadcasts') competitiveness. This creates the second paradox: ego and competitiveness result in sameness, rather than independent thought.

Often, individual reporters, particularly those from the major national media, have immense egos. Once Wright returned a phone call in the evening to ABC's Sam Donaldson. The ABC switchboard operator assumed that Donaldson would want to hear from the Speaker of the House who was returning his call and patched Wright through to Donaldson's home—but didn't say Wright was actually on the line. "I'm at home now," Donaldson said, evidently annoyed that the Speaker of the House presumed to disturb him there. "If he wants to talk to me he can call in the morning."

It is not only network superstars who have large egos. Reporters' egos, and the institutional egoism of the press, operates at every level. William Choyke was newly assigned to the Washington bureau of the *Fort Worth Star-Telegram* in 1977. He was twenty-seven years old, barely half Wright's age, and inexperienced in Washington. Wright, with twenty-two years in Congress, had just been elected majority leader of the House of Representatives. Recalling the time, Choyke said, "Here I was, fresh to Washington. Here he was, just elected majority leader. It was sort of like we were coming up together."

Edmund Burke, a member of parliament, may have been manipulating reporters himself when he called them "more important" than the members. In more recent history, no one played reporters' egos better than James Baker, Reagan's chief of staff and treasury secretary and George Bush senior's secretary of state. (Baker also was in charge of the strategy of George W. Bush in Florida to block a recount of votes out of fear that it would have made Al Gore president.) One reporter recalled, "I was writing something for a third-tier publication. Most people in Washington never heard of it. He gave me an interview. When I sat down he was on the phone, got off, apologized, and said, 'We won't be interrupted again for twenty minutes.' What he was really saying to me was, '*You're very important.*' You don't think I wasn't flattered?"

One of Baker's first acts after being named secretary of state, before meeting with career foreign service officials, was to host a reception for diplomatic reporters. When the stories finally did break about his conflict of interest—owning several million dollars of Chemical Bank while setting policy on Third World debt which protected the bank's interests— he escaped serious attack. Public pressure did at last force him to sell his stock, but a headline in the *Washington Post* read, "Action Said To Go 'Well Beyond' Ethics Rules." Soon the story died. On a TV talk show, veteran journalist Jack Germond marveled at how gentle reporters had been and concluded, "Only Jim Baker could walk away from this thing."

Reporters need strong egos; to do their job properly, they must not be intimidated by the powerful. But that same ego may allow them to be manipulated. If a cabinet secretary invites a reporter to breakfast, the following day's paper will frequently contain precisely the story the cabinet secretary wanted printed. The late CBS network anchor Eric Sevareid said flatly, "The press can be bought by leaks because of ego."

Competitive pressures add to the complex of ego. Except for professional athletes and coaches, journalists may compete more than members of any other profession. The *Wall Street Journal, New York Times*, and *Washington Post* compete incessantly. An outer circle of major papers tries to break through into the inner circle, including the *Los Angeles Times, Baltimore Sun, Boston Globe*, and even the *Washington Times*, which, although run by the "moonie" Unification Church, became important precisely because of its conservative bias. Similarly, *Time* and *Newsweek* compete, while *US News and World Report* tries to penetrate into the top tier. And each network newscast rating point translates into millions of dollars.

Reporters compete within their own organizations for time on a broadcast, and for a front-page story instead of a page-fifteen story. They dramatize the facts to win, or they highlight something that is relatively unimportant but attention-getting; sometimes this effectively distorts the story. Indeed, that eagerness to dramatize distorts the truth more than any ideological bias. Although conservatives routinely complain about liberal bias in the media, the Reagan administration, by far the most conservative since Calvin Coolidge, was much better treated than Carter, Ford, Nixon, or Johnson—not to mention Bush or Clinton. Deep into Reagan's presidency, then Vice President George Bush agreed that "the media has treated the administration pretty well."

What reporters care most about are good stories—what *Washington Post* editor Ben Bradlee called "Holy Shit!" stories, stories that wake people up, that get people's attention. Those are "good" stories.

The pressure to dramatize, or over-dramatize, a story is not the only problem generated by competitiveness. Another is shallowness. Most Washington journalists are highly intelligent, and yet few pursue stories in any depth; they do not spend enough time to learn something. Nor do they want to. While promoting his autobiography, Walter Cronkite, an icon in American journalism, said that his proudest achievement as a journalist was to beat the other networks by thirty seconds with getting the news that John F. Kennedy had been shot on the air.

Yet the most serious consequence of competitiveness is that it combines with the ego of reporters—and their insecurities, since their names are attached to their stories—to yield the opposite of what one might expect. Instead of dozens of independent and different assessments of the truth, the media moves toward a consensus view.

That consensus view begins with reporters, who are covering the same story, sitting next to each other on campaign planes, sharing facilities in the House and Senate press galleries, or compressed even closer together in the rabbit-warren press area of the White House. Reporters compare each other's notes of what someone said, which improves accuracy, but sometimes these conversations between journalists move to the next stage, if one reporter will say, or another ask, what he or she thinks the story lead is. A sameness develops. More importantly, reporters read each other's stories.

According to a *Wall Street Journal* study, every day 89 percent of Washington reporters read the *Post*, 73 percent read the *Times*, and 51 percent read the *Journal*; a significant minority also reads one or more of the second-tier papers such as the *Los Angeles Times*. The first day's stories of

an event often differ widely, as each writer pursues his or her own interpretation. But then inaccuracies can start to ripple through stories; reporters rarely check a "fact" which they see in another story. They simply repeat it. It becomes almost impossible to correct. A consensus view
ripples through stories, too, beginning to form on the third and fourth
day, partly because more facts are known but also because reporters,
having read competitors' stories, adjust their own, pull themselves back
into the crowd. Any reporter who takes a different line must justify
himself or herself to editors. James Doyle, former chief political correspondent for *Newsweek*, observes, "Your editor sees the AP lead, the
Washington Post lead, the *New York Times* lead. You have to have great
will-power and self-assurance to go in a different direction."

Reporters want to be first, but want others to follow. They want to
stand out, but be confirmed in their judgement. Jerry ter Horst, once
President Gerald Ford's press secretary and a former *Detroit News* bureau chief, said, "When I had an exclusive, I never wanted it to be exclusive very long. I'd call friends in the wires to push it."

The cluster of reporters hounding after one story resembles what
Nobel laureate Elias Canetti described as a "pack" in his book *Crowds
and Power*: "In the changing constellation of the pack, in its dances and
expeditions, [a member of a pack] will again and again find himself at its
edge. He may be at the center, and then, immediately afterwards, at the
edge again.... They are not a multitude and have to make up in intensity
what they lack in actual numbers.... I am here deliberately opposing all
the usual concepts of tribe, sib, clan.... Those well-known sociological
concepts...stand for something static. The pack, in contrast, is a unit
for *action*.... The truest and most natural pack is that from which our
word derives, the hunting pack."

The press resembles Canetti's "crowd" as well on major stories. Then
editorial writers and columnists begin to echo the primary reporters on
a story, and editors take reporters off other beats and assign them to the
first one. The crowd becomes denser, more pack-like, both in numbers
and in interpretation as each journalist's story becomes influenced by
his colleagues' and all the stories become more and more alike.

Canetti wrote, "The most important occurrence within a crowd is...
the moment when all who belong to the crowd get rid of their differences and feel equal.... Before this the crowd does not exist. The crowd

needs a direction. . . . Its constant fear of disintegration means that it will accept any goal."

The press is a force, all right, but it has no direction of its own, no goal. It takes its direction from the outside. The crowd, and the press, follows. Ten years after leaving the White House, Jimmy Carter observed, "When a president is running high and has favorable reaction in the public opinion polls, he's also treated with kid gloves and deference by the press. If he starts going down though, then he's condemned by the press."

The direction of the press can be turned, abruptly, through a single dramatic event—a breakthrough in international peace, or an explosive new policy, or a scandal. It can also be steered, more gradually, like an ocean liner being guided into a berth by a more broad-based circumstance. A continued economic recession or period of growth can dictate its tone.

In those cases, the press reflects fundamental realities outside itself, in the same way a stock's price will ultimately reflect the underlying value of a company. But the press can also depart from realities, just as the stock market may indulge in speculative or fearful frenzies about the future of a stock. The difference between the press and the market is that the press has much more ability to create a self-fulfilling prophecy. *Power is perception. One who is believed to have power does.*

And Canetti identified what he called "crowd crystals," which, like larger events, also have the power to generate and direct crowds. He described crowd crystals as "the small, rigid groups of men, strictly delimited and of great constancy, which serve to precipitate crowds. Their structure is such that they can be comprehended and taken in at a glance. Their unity is more important than their size. Their role must be familiar; people must know what they are there for. . . . The crowd crystal is *constant*; it never changes its size. Its members are trained in both action and faith. . . . The clarity, isolation, and constancy of the crystal form an uncanny contrast with the excited flux of the surrounding crowd. . . . The return of the moment when they are needed is as certain as the appearance of new crowds. Individual crowd crystals precipitate crowds."

Gingrich had a theme. He understood the media well, and played reporters' egos, too. He introduced more than one journalist to other congressmen by calling them, "One of the most serious, intelligent, and solid reporters there is covering Congress."

He also understood what made a "good" story and how he could use the media's desire for drama. "The number-one fact about the news media is that they love fights," Gingrich had said. "When you give them confrontations you get attention."

Gingrich had a strategy. And every single message he sent out either directly or indirectly reflected it. He would become his own crowd crystal.

The crowd needs a direction. Its constant fear of disintegration means that it will accept any goal.

GAME'S OVER

Football involves a different kind of power. Physical force, mental toughness and resilience, matched against that of an opponent. But the outside world intervenes here, too. Both the game and the world can just wear one down. Or they can create real tragedy.

Unlike most of the rest of the book, I was directly involved in what I write about here. The first story in this section originally appeared in Sports Illustrated. I was living in Rhode Island then, and had decided to do a story about a game at every level of football—youth, high school, small college, major college, and the NFL—and about what remained the same and what changed as the game went from level to level. I never wrote that story. When I watched the Patriots play, their quarterback got hurt. It started me thinking about injuries. I wrote the story included here. It was the first piece I ever sold to a national magazine.

Normally I write slowly, and labor over every word. But both this story and "Jimmy" earlier in the book were written in one sitting of fifteen or twenty minutes each. Apparently I was just ready to write them.

The second piece originally ran in the Washington Post Magazine. At the time I didn't think it had anything to do with Washington. But now in the context of this book, and in the context of the final piece in this section, I think maybe it did.

IT'S ALL A PART OF
THE GAME

Recently I watched New England Patriots quarterback Jim Plunkett, the former Heisman trophy winner, go down with an injury that required surgery, and then listened as another Patriots player was asked about it. "It's part of the game," he said. "You know? You can't worry about going down. It's part of the game."

Football coaches become inured to players getting hurt, even though the coaches are as vulnerable to injuries as the players. After all, it can mean coaches' jobs and coaches' careers. When I coached, I waved aside images of players going under the knife. I had to. But now, when a player lies on the ground I go get a hot dog, or turn away from the television set for one or two or three minutes, and try not to think about the one boy I saw get really hurt. I'm not a coach anymore and I do think about it.

I went down myself as a player; pain shot up my leg and I was wincing instead of running. My recovery progressed slowly. I believed the coaches all thought I was dogging it, but, damn it, I wasn't. At first the sideways glances the coaches shot at me made me feel guilty, but later I grew so angry that I decided never to play again.

The next season found me in the stands, but watching gnawed and gnawed at me. Not so much the not playing. It was more that I felt like a quitter, which is far worse than being just a loser. That feeling continued to haunt me after graduation until I scrapped my Ivy League degree and graduate-school fellowship and nascent doctoral dissertation to coach a high school team. Of course, I swore always to give a player the benefit of the doubt on any injury.

Like every other high school coach, when a boy went down I would run onto the field and order players to move back and ask, "Where's it hurt?" and hope someone who actually knew something about injuries would come out on the field. Quick.

During one game at a private school in the South the smallest player on the field, one of those fast, tough kids with a great heart you always see in high school athletics, the kind of kid you love, went down. Out cold. I ran out there with a doctor. The boy was not badly hurt, the doctor said, and could even return to the game, so after he rested I sent him back in. We needed him in there.

But in the locker room after the game the boy collapsed. He lay on the floor unconscious, his eyes glassy, sweating profusely.

I raced out of the locker room to find the doctor. While waiting for the ambulance—the one at the game had left already—I slammed my fist against the lockers and shouted, "That *doctor* said he could play! Where's that *doctor?*" I felt guilt and wanted to transfer that guilt to him; I felt hate and wanted to kill him. The boy, as it turned out, was fine and later in the season even played again.

I was successful enough in high school, then coached football at a small college and finally joined the staff at Tulane University. Fantasyland for someone who didn't even play three years of Ivy League football. But it wasn't the sauna in the locker room or the 80,000-seat home stadium that struck me as so different. It was the zippers. So many athletes had zippers down the side of their knee, or knees; they thought nothing of it and called this or that a "Band-Aid" operation. I just kept looking at where the knife had cut and shaking my head. There were so many who had had surgery.

In college the coaches don't deal directly with injuries. There are trainers for that. In college the coaches receive injury reports and worry about them. "Oh, Christ," they mutter when someone lies a little too long on the ground. "Get up. You're not hurt. Damn it, don't be hurt."

"It's not too bad," the trainer says. "Have to cut sometime, but not right now. You never know. He might make it through the whole season."

When the season ends, those injured players who did make it through the year check into the hospital for surgery. The sooner the better for all concerned. The players are as anxious as the coaches; spring practice is not that far away. I remember thinking how odd one thing was: one freshman had made the varsity that more than half a million adults had paid to cheer. He was under eighteen so the hospital put him in the kiddies' ward and decorated his walls with flappy-eared purple elephants. He did not take kindly to his surroundings. He's an orthopedic surgeon himself now.

It's a cold business all right. In preseason we were running a game-type scrimmage inside our huge empty stadium, referees and all. A wide receiver runs an out. The quarterback ducks a rushing linebacker and starts to run, is chased, crosses the line of scrimmage. The receiver's eyes gleam, a pursuing defensive tackle all picked out, and he sets himself to unload a blind-side shot, to clean that guy's clock. Except it isn't blind side. The defensive tackle sees him coming and—WHAM!—he does the unloading on the receiver, running full-speed at him, and the receiver goes down, stumbles to his feet, goes down again and stays on the ground. Out run the trainers. Out runs a substitute receiver. The boy went down in front of the defensive bench. The defensive coaches ignore him. Hell, he's a receiver. He's not one of theirs. The offensive coaches are huddled, engrossed in play selection. The trainers help the boy off the field.

The head coach, Benny Ellender, approaches the offensive coaches, beckons one of them closer.

"Don't you *ever*," he says, "don't you *ever* let a boy lie on the ground again without a coach going over to him."

The season started and the team was doing well, winning games and staying pretty healthy. One starter did get hurt, though, and had to have his knee operated on, for the third time. He'd have been a pro prospect but for those operations. A couple of days after the surgery we were playing a night game at home. I knew no players would visit him that day— on game days the players had to stay in the athletic dorm for meetings and taping and eating and just being together. I thought the player would feel like the forgotten man, so in the afternoon, when I had nothing to do really but watch whatever game was on TV, I decided to visit him myself. Another visitor was there when I arrived. The head coach, Ellender. You wouldn't catch many head coaches out visiting a player, except maybe a high school All-American, the day of a game. I always liked that man.

When I think of football injuries I like to think of incidents like that, like Ellender on game day visiting the boy in the hospital. And to forget a day I can't forget. I was coaching the defense at Providence College,

TIME OUT: INJURY

Five college football players who have been sidelined, some for the entire season, discuss what it feels like: the sudden sense of vulnerability; the psychological trauma; the frustration of no longer being a part of the team.

JAY MILLER, BRIGHAM YOUNG, WR
Torn knee ligaments

"You freak, you freaky thing," I said to my knee when I reinjured it. I couldn't believe it. "This is Jay Miller," I thought, "the guy who caught a hundred passes in a season. The guy who was invincible, who could never be hurt." It humbles me. As a sophomore I was a hero, but last year I was hurt for most of the season and now I'm nothing. When I see someone else on the field, cutting for a pass on a healthy knee, I look at my cast, and I'm just plain envious. Football is still my dream, but now I know I'm vulnerable like the next guy. One Saturday you're leaving on a plane while the cheerleaders wave goodby, and then suddenly you're like the rest of the students.

CARL HUBBARD, AUBURN, LB
Slipped disk; separated shoulder; knee

I've undergone so much medical treatment my teammates call me the $6 Million Man. I've missed sixteen games and once I even thought about quitting, but I've always come back. I attend all the meetings and prepare for a game mentally just as if I were going to play. During the game I'm on the sidelines, trying to give moral support or spot mistakes. You have to be involved. It's been tougher on me, but I've gotten more out of football because of it. I'm more invincible now than ever before. People wonder if it's worth the risk of not being able to walk again. It sure is. I've found that playing college football is the best thing in the world. No price is too great.

DAVE ZUMBACH, BOSTON COLLEGE, WR
Severely bruised kneecap

I don't know what to do. I don't even feel like part of the team anymore. I'm just hobbling on crutches, on the outside looking in. I was never a very confident person, anyway, and now the confidence football had given me has drained. When you've been a player and all of a sudden you're not, it's a pretty shattering experience. It's affected my personality and my relationships with other people and, I'm afraid, my pro chances. I cut classes, feeling sorry for myself. That's bad because everybody else seems to feel sorry for me, too. But this thing preys on my mind. It's my senior year and I think I'm letting folks down. I feel funny even being in the locker room.

KIRK LEWIS, MICHICAN, RG
Broken forearm

After years of building up my body I felt I had conditioned myself against injury. When my arm broke so easily, it amazed me. I wondered why it hadn't happened before. I still haven't recovered from that psychologically. The possibility of permanent damage also bothers me because I hope to be a surgeon someday. I never knew how much I liked football until I sat out our opening game against Wisconsin. Being on the sidelines made me sick in the pit of my stomach. I'll never forget that feeling. One thing I don't miss is the constant pressure and mental strain. It's like a great weight has been lifted from my shoulders. I don't have to perform.

DAVE FARMER, USC, FB
Broken leg

While they were carting me off the field after my injury I was beating my fists against my thigh pads yelling "Why me? Why me?" And I was crying like heck, not because it hurt but because it wiped out everything I'd been working so hard for. Pain is part of football. I seem to love it. But I was afraid I'd blown my chance to show the pros what I could do. Now that I'm on crutches, I'm the slowest man on campus. I've had trouble sleeping, but with this extra time I've added a new course. After the game Coach [John] McKay told me I had come far and would be back again. You'd better believe I will. My outlook hasn't changed, only my time frame.

very small-time football. (Big-time basketball; the PC basketball team went to the Final Four that year, but small-time football.) But for our level the team was excellent. Even though it was November, we had not lost a game. Naturally the team we were playing was up, whooping and hollering and jumping up and down on each other's toes and in general doing all sorts of carrying-on before the game. We went through our warm-ups with a minimum of screeching, poised as always. The other team was screaming louder than ever at the opening kickoff, on which our two-hundred-pound return man took the ball out to about the 30, near our sideline. I saw the hit that brought him down. It was not a particularly hard tackle, but the other team shouted, "Good stick! Good stick!" just the same, and a couple of their players hustled over to pat the tackler as he got up. Except he didn't get up. He had gone down.

Their trainer ran out there, with the other team's coaches, talking to him. He wasn't moving. Our trainer ran out.

"For Chrissakes," I was thinking. "Get up, kid."

Our head coach came over to me. "Really playing the role out there, huh?"

"Yeah."

Then the other team's trainer yelled for the doctor.

The doctor? Maybe the kid was hurt after all. We looked for the doctor. No doctor. The boy had been on the field for close to five minutes now. The trainer asked a cop to call the rescue squad. Where the hell was an ambulance? No doctor, no ambulance.

The doctor arrived. We weren't paying him. He was a volunteer. He thought it was a 2:00 game, not 1:30. Sorry.

Now rumors spread along our bench that the kid was dead. I turned around and tongue-lashed a player who said that. "Don't be a jerk. Look at him. He's talking to the doctor."

Sirens. The rescue truck digging tracks in the moist field. Ten minutes had passed since the kid went down. I finally decided to join the huddle around the boy and see if we could get things moving.

With his helmet off, he looked shrunken and fragile in his equipment, his head sticking out of the massive shoulder pads like that of a small boy from his father's much-too-large jacket. He looked frightened. The doctor leaned over him.

"Am I going to be all right? I'm going to be all right, aren't I?"

"Just relax now."

"I can't feel anything. My legs. I can't feel anything." His voice, a scared child's voice. A lost child's voice. Wanting to be found. His face was handsome, almost pretty. The trainer took the boy's cleats and socks off.

"Can you move your toes?"

The boy's face strained and tensed, his teeth grated and his eyes closed as he bore down, and a little sweat appeared on his face. The toes did not move.

"Can you feel this?" The trainer jabbed a scissors' tip into his foot.

"What did you say?" the boy asked.

The trainer looked up, as if appealing to me. "Oh . . . nothing," he told the boy.

As all the people bustled around the boy, he asked again, "Am I going to be all right? I can't feel my legs."

The doctor said they were taking him to the hospital, that one of the best neurosurgeons in the country, from Brown University, would see him, as if the boy should feel honored, as if the fact that the neurosurgeon taught at Brown University made him omniscient and omnipotent.

Our offensive team was on the field running through plays. Their defense was doing calisthenics. It was not cold for the season, but it was November, and they had to stay warm or risk muscle pulls. I looked at the boy's face, at the wonderment in it, and felt sick. Sick of football. It couldn't be worth it. His eyes were open wide, as if absorbing this world never seen before. They started cutting off his equipment and he closed his eyes briefly, then reopened them.

"Am I going to be all right?" he asked the doctor one last time.

"Yes," the doctor answered him, "you're going to be fine."

Although he was already lying flat on the ground he seemed to lean back then, or sort of settle. I stood off to the side with our head coach, watching knives slash through pads. We had loaned our opponents some equipment before the game; their managers had screwed up their preparations and had forgotten to pack some pads. "With our luck," somebody said, "those are our pads they're cutting through."

I laughed. It was funny. I turned away from the semicircle of people gathered around the boy and tried not to laugh; put my hand over my mouth and still laughed. It was funny. We had had budget problems all year.

They weren't our pads. We won the game easily, our fifth shutout of the season. The boy was paralyzed. I continued to coach for another three years before I quit. During that time I had players in the hospital and never got around to visiting them. Too busy planning practices. And after all, you can't worry about going down. It's part of the game.

NO MORE PLAY

L ate each summer all the NFL teams start to make their final cuts, and the game will be over for some players. Being treated like children, being told to be at lunch, in bed at a certain time, all those things will be over. With that will also go the chance of serious money, but most athletes, even the most professional among them, will say that performance doesn't depend on the money. In sport—it can be different in business, where psyches get involved in different ways—the pursuit of money alone is a rational thing, and to play at your peak you must tap into more primal feelings. What makes a player endure the pain, emotional and physical, of playing can be many things. It may be the need to dominate, to prove you are better. It may be the fear of not surviving. It may be the love of your teammates, and the need not to let them down and have them respect you. It may be the adulation of the crowds. It may be the sheer joy and absolute freedom of *play*. Regardless, all those things will be gone too. If the cut players haven't grown up yet—a lot haven't—they will have to in a hurry. Pro sports is a suspension of time, but there is no chance for decompression.

Athletes put their identities on the line in a way most of us don't. They are taught to compete, that only winning counts, that failure is like dying. So what happens when they do fail? When they have to move on?

Three friends had to confront that failure. I know them because I coached them. Once 86,958 people watched a team where I was an assistant, Tulane University, play LSU. At the time it was the largest crowd ever to see a football game in the South, college or pro, bowl game or Super Bowl, although since then Tennessee has expanded its stadium. It was a great LSU team, one that had been ranked number five in the country and had lost only one game, to number one Alabama, and went to the Orange Bowl. Our Tulane team was the best in twenty-five years, also nationally ranked.

Tulane hadn't beaten LSU in twenty-five years either. We won 14–0. I remember how the stadium shook when we scored, how one part of the stadium was absolutely still. I remember everything about the game, from running out for warm ups in the brittle December night air to how the lights made it all seem surreal, how we designed the option so Foley would keep the ball, how...everything. Maybe I haven't exactly moved on myself.

DEMARS

Ted DeMars could run fast, cut fast, and bowl people over. Not quite six feet tall and just about two hundred pounds, he had thick legs and wide shoulders which belied his grace. Once at Classical High School in Providence, where I coached him, playing against a good team, he carried the ball just five times and scored on runs of twenty-five, sixty, and—the first play of the game—seventy-five yards. In track he sprinted and put the shot over sixty feet, an extraordinary feat for a running back and a sign of his explosiveness. (By comparison, 6'7", 330-pound Baltimore Ravens All-Pro offensive tackle Jonathan Ogden, the highest paid lineman in the NFL, would have beaten DeMars by four inches in the shot put.) DeMars was All State in three sports, High School All American in one, with good grades. And of course his initials spelled T.D.

He came into his own in the final game of his junior season. It was a losing year but we jelled two-thirds the way through it, ruining the otherwise perfect record of the league champion and starting a win streak of our own. In the final game you could see that DeMars had *gotten* it, that he suddenly understood his own special abilities and began to make use of them. It came together for him on one play, an eighty-six-yard touchdown. There was a hole, he saw it and accelerated cleanly through it, ran right over one defender who tried to tackle him, cut for the open, and outran everyone else. It was a mental thing. Until that play he had never quite had confidence in his abilities; before then it had seemed as if he figured if the linebacker had a clean shot he should be tackled and so he....I don't know how to put it, but it was almost as if he allowed himself to be tackled.

Once he had gotten it, he didn't lose it. I remember an intrasquad scrimmage in preseason practice his senior season when our best linebacker did have a clean shot at him, popped him really hard, but DeMars just shrugged him off and kept going. The linebacker got up and looked at me, puzzled and shaking his head. I smiled.

We went undefeated that year. Our team had tremendous character, tremendous intensity. No one on that team needed to be led. They were all leaders, except for DeMars himself. We didn't have an offensive lineman over 185 pounds but they were all athletes, including a High School All American in track, a state pole vault champion, and two others who played college baseball. Our fullback was the biggest player on the team, and he started in college at defensive tackle. So DeMars wasn't the only good player. He was just the best. He was also definitely the least intense, the least determined.

He never made a big deal about scoring. He never made a big deal about anything. He just accepted his own ability and used it, never worked with weights, never trained in the off-season. But if he seemed to lack the kind of direction or determination usually associated with success, he had an extraordinary sense of self.

He was not a leader, not a follower, not a loner. He was simply himself. It was a passive trait. He was going to do what he was going to do. He would not be aroused. If he didn't want to do something, neither logic nor pressure could make him do it.

When he was a high school junior he began dating a twenty-seven-year-old woman. They held hands after games, and he would chuckle, as he always did. It was a scandal. People urged him to break up. His teachers took him aside. His coaches took him aside. His friends took him aside. At least, they said, don't be so public. He just shook his head and shook off their interference. Fourteen years later he and the woman still are together.

Football nurtured that sense of self, too. He says, "I just loved the thrill of the game. Not even the game. Just running with the ball and having everyone chase me. The fact they were after me, I liked it—that I was the center, the focal point, and nobody else. It's just a great feeling."

He could have gone to any school in the country. He chose Harvard. In the fourth game his sophomore year he went seventy-five yards for a score against Dartmouth. Every game after that he started. His junior year he made first team All Conference. The other All Conference running back was Ed Marinaro, runner-up for the Heisman Trophy, who spent many years in the NFL with the Vikings. His senior year he made first team All Conference again. This time the other running back was Dick Jauron, who became a star defensive back with the Chicago Bears. Ted finished his career as Harvard's number two all-time leading scorer and rusher. And he was captain.

His selection as captain surprised me. It surprised him, too. Later he told me, laughing, "Hey, I'm one of toughest guys on the team."

He was not bragging about that fact. We both knew he hadn't been close to the toughest—tough in the sense of grit and determination—on the Classical team. We both knew he was saying that if he was one of the toughest, it wasn't a very tough team. But he was reliable. He certainly would always perform. As I said before, he was going to do what he was going to do.

To captain a Harvard football team gives one a tremendous entree— business, law, even politics. The doors were there. DeMars never went through them, because of, he says, "Uncertainty. I wasn't really sure what I wanted to do."

So while essentially marking time he played more football, on a minor league pro team. Six members of his team made the NFL the following year, and he was named both the team's and the league's Most Valuable Player. The next year saw the emergence of the World Football League, which after it folded sent many coaches and players to the NFL. Prominent NFL stars signed with the new league. The New York Stars offered a good contract. DeMars signed.

He was full of surprises. The second fastest back in camp, he caught the ball very, very well and ran good patterns. Even at that level his power broke tackles and his cuts found open space. Up and up he moved on the depth charts. So he surprised everyone again when he walked out of camp.

He says simply, "I always like the informality of football, the freedom of the sandlot. The more it got structured the less I liked it. Of course, the farther up you go, the more structured it gets. It was inevitable that I wasn't going to make it."

He didn't know what he wanted. So he went into the woods alone and looked for something to want. When he came out he said he wanted some land. Or a boat. Yeah, a boat he could live on. That was what he wanted.

I was coaching a high school team in Florida and asked him to be my assistant. He asked, laughing, "Is it near the water?" Whenever I tried to talk about split-six defenses or loaded options, he said, "Whatever you want, you're the head coach." Then he'd borrow one of the player's surfboards and hit the beach.

He didn't like coaching—structure again. He did like to run pass patterns. It got to be where the players would double- and triple-team him, interfere illegally, but he always got open and if the ball was anywhere near him, he caught it. And once when we were working on punt coverage he returned a punt. He had no blockers and the first string, some good players, went downfield to cover; they weren't trying to tackle him, just touch him.

Not one could. He scored.

I had coached both small and major college football by then and had been exposed to many players who did well in the NFL. He looked as good as anyone I had ever seen. I told him to go back to the pros. I might even be able to help, with some calls to people I knew.

He glanced off somewhere and a second later just said, "Nah."

I left that school and he was offered the head coaching job. He declined. Nor did he coach anywhere else. He returned to New England. In the Rhode Island state lottery he won what, adjusting for inflation, would be about $75,000 in the year 2000.

It was actually the second prize, awarded at a big publicized dinner where a few finalists awaited the drawing for the grand prize. The grand prize was that same amount every year for life. Practically everyone else I know, certainly including myself, would be haunted—at least a little— by how close they had come to the grand prize. Ted didn't think that way. He was happy with what he had gotten.

He thought he'd buy a neighborhood bar, just a place to hang out. But there wasn't enough for that, so he ended up buying a house and a couple of acres halfway between Hartford and Providence. He lives there, with his girlfriend.

For a year he worked for the lieutenant governor of Rhode Island. For two years he worked in an alternative sentencing program. He felt he was accomplishing something and liked it, but finally got fed up with bureaucracy and hearing lies told and quit. He got a boat, finally, to dig up quahaugs commercially. But that didn't pay as well as he expected. In the winter he sells firewood off his land, but there isn't a whole lot. He makes Tiffany lamps and sells them. For a while he talked about law school, but he's thirty-one now and doesn't talk about it anymore.

I visited him not too long ago. We talked about old times. He chuckled about the punt return in Florida: "I felt like Jim Thorpe." Then we took a whiffle ball and bat into the yard.

I had never beaten him in anything athletic and wouldn't give him a strike now. He swung and missed, and laughed. Swung and popped the ball up, and laughed. Then he concentrated. The next pitch was well out of the strike zone and up near his head, but this time he stepped away from it and still swung. The ball took off, sailed, landed way back in the trees.

As I went after it, he warned, "Watch out. There's poison ivy in there. I remember worrying about poison ivy when I was a kid."

He paused then, kicked around in the brush, and said, "Of course, I'm not a kid anymore, am I?"

WEEKS

Brian Weeks seems kind of stolid, and slow. But Weeks is easy to underestimate. He has a way of saying things—even if crudely—that pierces. About his former coach at the New England Patriots, Chuck Fairbanks, he snorts, "He's so slick his shit doesn't stink."

More importantly, he got where he was going, almost always. He succeeded through intensity and work. In practice he worked every day on every play to learn something, trying to make a better read, trying to improve his technique, experimenting with different moves, different stances. A handful of times in four years in college, lining up against a close friend, he would fool around, and then stay up at night feeling guilty. He considers his football career like "the Protestant ethic. I always figured I worked harder than the other guy, so I deserved to win."

Weeks is 6'5" and weighed about 235 pounds. He played defensive tackle at Providence College, which then played on the absolute lowest level of college football and no longer plays any football at all. But I was defensive coordinator there for two years. My first year we allowed only forty-six points all season and shut out five teams. My second year we allowed forty-two points. It was a long way from big-time football, but when I went to Tulane I tried to get Weeks to accept a scholarship there for his last two years. He was paying his own way at PC. He wouldn't come. Loyalty. A year later, thinking of exposure to the pros and challenging himself against better players, he did walk on at the University of Massachusetts and in three practices rose from dead last on the depth chart, the number fourteen defensive tackle, to number three, but felt too guilty about leaving his teammates and returned to PC.

His senior year he not only starred, as usual, on defense, but returned punts. Not too many defensive tackles are punt returners, on any level. In fact I never heard of another one, except maybe as a joke when a team was ahead 50–0. Weeks did it for real. He wasn't much gifted when it came to making a cut, but he had speed and balance, could run over a few people, and he caught the ball well.

The Patriots wanted him to play linebacker. Linebackers cover backs running pass routes. I doubted that he had the athletic ability required for pass defense but didn't say so. He was fast enough but not agile enough, and agility is one thing that intensity cannot compensate for.

Anyway, the Patriots signed him to a free-agent contract the day after the draft in 1975, while elsewhere in the same offices they were introducing their number one draft choice and later All Pro, Russ Francis, to a room packed with media folks. Weeks wasn't mentioned, not even as a footnote in a press release. On the field, he and Francis would be lining up head to head. No doubt Francis was unaware of that. But Weeks was aware.

Brian Weeks wanted to make it more than most people dare to want anything. He explains why: "You don't get many weak egos on the field, though you do find an occasional coward. You line up your face masks and one guy says, 'I'm gonna kick your ass.' My approach was, let the other guy start it, and I'll finish it. I liked it. That, and you bleed with other guys. You build bonds. I would enjoy a sweep on my end, and I'd hit the guy high and Brady would come in low, then we'd pick each other up. That feeling, there's nothing like it on earth."

He wanted it to continue so he worked. Handball for quickness two or three times a week, for months; weights for strength and weight gain three or four times a week, for months. Given my own background with weights, I designed his lifting program and often worked out with him. He ate, and ate, and ate, and gained weight. He ran, and ran, and ran, and increased his stamina and speed.

I went to watch a mini-camp practice in April. As a warm-up drill, everyone on the team had to catch punts catapulted out of a machine. Weeks was the only player, including the veterans, who didn't drop any. But catching a football is largely a matter of concentration. I never doubted his ability to focus. He still showed me nothing that made me think he could succeed as a linebacker.

Then there was nothing more to do. Before leaving for training camp he told me, "If it comes down to me or another guy, one on one, I can't conceive of not making it." He shook his head. "I just can't conceive of it."

The first full-go scrimmage, he was lined up on Francis and Shelby Jordan, a solid first-string tackle. Weeks remembers, "I wanted to get ready for a good crack. I whacked myself on the helmet a couple of times." The play came right at him. Francis exploded on him, driving, driving. Weeks rammed his shoulder under Francis' chin and tried to get free. Then Jordan was on him. "Then the ball carrier. It was boom-boom-boom."

He split the double-team of an All-Pro tight end and a starting NFL tackle. His voice resonates with satisfaction. "I got him for a couple-yard loss. God! God it felt good! I got up and saw the coach. He was looking straight at me. Didn't say anything. Then he sort of nodded."

Brian laughs. "Goddam, it felt good."

But he had played defensive tackle all his life, not linebacker. And it did not come down to a him-or-me in a head-to-head fist-fight type situation. It was him or me in who had the quickest feet, the ability to stay with a receiver, the quickest reaction to the ball. He had never covered a pass receiver in his life, and the NFL was not a great place to begin. He was cut. Coming from a school as small as Providence, trying a position he had never played, he had very few other opportunities. No other NFL team picked him up.

It wasn't over, though. Fairbanks left the Patriots after that season and his staff scrambled for jobs. The coach who had nodded to Weeks after he split the double team moved to the Toronto Argonauts. Toronto signed Weeks. He spent another year lifting and running. He and I worked on his pass drops.

He was in the Toronto training room one day soaking in ice when someone walked by with his jersey. He went out on the field to find out why, though he knew why, and says, "I was crying when I walked off. Getting cut by the Patriots was traumatic, but I knew I'd get another chance. This time, though, I knew it was my last time on the field as a player. It's the worst feeling on earth."

He elaborates. "Let me tell you what it felt like, being cut. It's like a death in the family. Like your father died, if you're close to your father. Only it's worse. It's worse because you have the sense that you could have prevented it. You could have saved him. If only you had worked harder, done more, been smarter. It's like he died because you failed. You live with that every day."

Today Weeks sells wallets to department stores and lives in Harvard, Massachusetts. His football is limited to reminiscing—his eyes fire up then.

Brian Weeks was twenty-eight the last time I saw him, two years ago. He was the leading salesman in the country for his company, always working hard, always following up, always prepared, and now he manages sales for the Northeast. He had just married his high school sweetheart. He should have been happy. But football had done something to him.

"I think it's colder than business and I think business is colder than hell," he says. "But I love it. Playing football was clearly the best time of my life. The best time I'll ever have.

"I don't dwell on it. It doesn't pay the bills. It doesn't make the dog happy. It doesn't make Tricia happy. But I feel I let my parents down. I feel I let you down. I feel I let the program at Providence down. I feel I let myself down. I feel those things. I don't dwell on it. But I can still taste it."

THIBODEAUX

Tom Thibodeaux played tight end at Tulane and was drafted by the Saints. He was once described by a sportswriter as "a brute of a man, often accused of savage instincts on the field." Neither description was true, although he was a hitter and played football with intensity.

He seemed dark and brooding and had a sharp, intolerant tongue. He did not suffer fools lightly, wanted to know why if a coach told him to do something, and liked to thumb his nose at rules. On sweeps he often held his man illegally, but he had devised a technique the refs could not detect. It wasn't so much cheating, just his private game, a way of saying, "Ha! Try and catch me!" He was not enamored of either authority or coaches, nor they of him. His ability forced them to tolerate him.

Personally I always liked him. I had no problem with his attitude, as long as he played hard. Maybe one reason I liked him is that I'm not keen on respecting rules or people in authority either. Respect has to be earned. It doesn't come with a position.

At Tulane, I had not been at spring practice so all the players saw me for the first time when preseason practice began, and on the second or third day of practice I was supposed to work with the tight ends on a particular blocking technique. I had little authority to begin with. In addition, I'm 5'9" tall. Everyone else was at least 6'2" and most were taller. (I used to forget that I was short. Once I recall walking with a handful of players past a window and seeing all of our reflections and wondering, *who's that little guy next to Charley Hall*, then realizing, the little guy was me.)

It was clear Thibodeaux was going to test me. I taught the technique and was correcting a player who was too aggressive—this particular block had to be maintained for a long time, and even if an aggressive block knocked the defender back, he would have time to recover and make the play. Thibodeaux must have liked what I said since he suddenly declared himself on my side. "That's a pussy block," he said, "but it works."

Through the season we got to know each other a little. Once I was up in the players' dorm and he wanted to arm-wrestle me. I wasn't a fool and agreed to do so only if he would in turn agree to finger-wrestle, when you enmesh each other's fingers in your own and try to bend back the other guy's fingers until he gives. I believed I'd have an advantage there; lifting, constantly picking up hundreds of pounds, had given me an unusually strong grip.

We arm-wrestled first, with a dozen players watching. I was grunting and my face was squeezed tight with effort. He seemed struggling, too. I was holding my own, surprising myself and them. Then suddenly he yawned, smiled, and slammed my arm to the table. He had been toying with me.

Now it was my turn. We stood up, held our hands out, and enmeshed our fingers. I wasn't going to give in, period, even if he broke all of my fingers. But my hunch turned out right. My grip was stronger than his. Pain is involved, too. When you succeed in bending someone else's fingers back, it hurts. Finally he said, "Okay. OKAY!" I let go and he opened and closed his fists and worked his fingers to return feeling to them. We were of course buddies after that.

Later I recall sitting with an NFL scout watching film of him in game. He was trying to block somebody who had stunted away from him—who on the snap of the ball had taken a predetermined first step in the opposite direction. Thibodeaux managed to recover and get his body on the defender. The scout nodded approvingly, "A lot of guys in the NFL couldn't do that."

Tom was drafted in the middle rounds. Like Weeks, though, the Saints wanted him to change positions, from tight end to guard. As a tight end he had good size, 6'3" 245 pounds. But as an interior offensive lineman he was small. He was a fighter all right, but still....

The Saints trained in Florida, not far from where I coached with Ted DeMars. We went to visit him. When Thibodeaux opened the door, he practically hugged me. But it wasn't me so much he was glad to see—it was more that I represented the outside world. Things weren't going so well for him, and he was glad to be reminded of another reality.

Ted and I and Tom and his roommate traded stories for a time. Then all of a sudden Thibodeaux got up, walked over to the door, and said, "The coaches don't like me."

His voice sounded weary, like that of a man who was tiring of the battle. There was confusion and bitterness.

"Coaches never liked you before," I reminded him. "Why should they start now?"

He laughed at that and seemed to feel better. "Yeah," he said. "I guess." Then he sat down on the bed and continued, "This isn't like college. They beat the hell out of you here."

He rolled up his pants. The flesh of his calf was discolored and gashed. Stitches held the flesh together. He probed it with his finger the way a small boy might test a flame's heat, and said, "Hey. It hurts."

He was angry, and angriest at himself, that he was taking things now that he would never have taken before. I knew his contract was a good one, and I knew he had said he was playing only for the money. But he wouldn't take those things for money. And it was pointless. He was good, maybe good enough, but not so good that coaches needed him, that they would tolerate any antics because of his ability or take the time to work with him and develop his talent fully. And they didn't like him.

He recalled that just the day before he had thrown a terrific block, and snorted, "The coach went crazy. He was jumping up and down screaming, 'Great lick, Gilbert! Great job, Gilbert!' I turned around and said, 'That wasn't Gilbert. It was Thibodeaux.' He just called the next play. Didn't say a word."

Neither did we for a minute. Then DeMars chuckled and said, "I guess it wasn't such a great block after all."

It doesn't sound that funny now, but all four of us cracked up. We were laughing so hard tears literally rolled down my cheeks.

Thibodeaux got cut later that season. The only time I've seen him since was a few years later at Tulane. Spring practice was ending with what was billed as a Varsity-Alumni game.

By then the Tulane coaching staff had changed. The head coach when I was there had been Benny Ellender. We had won nine, lost two, and beat LSU 14–0, gone to a bowl game, and got as high as number eleven in the national rankings. That was the best team Tulane had had since 1948. At the end of the season Ellender won numerous regional and one national coach of the year awards, and Tulane gave him a brand-new ten-year contract. Two years later Tulane fired him. Only one of his assistants was retained by the new coach.

In this spring game, the "Varsity" was the first two varsity strings, and the "Alumni" was really the third, fourth, and fifth varsity strings, with just about eleven alumni on each offense and defense thrown in. But every alumnus had been on that great team of a few years before. And now they were on the field again.

They even practiced, at first in groups—defensive ends over here, running backs (both of them) over there, the one quarterback throwing passes to receivers running routes against the one defensive back who showed up at practice. But then the one assistant left over from the old staff said, all right, let's run a few plays. And the offense formed a huddle (of ten men, less than half of whom had been first-stringers). Suddenly they were together, had been through it all together, and for a moment they were a team again. The huddle was fun but it was football too, business, and quick quick slick slick they ran plays. One player took off his helmet. "I always hated my helmet," he said. A wide receiver took his off too. "I have a headache already. I always thought the headaches were from hitting." He rubbed his forehead and laughed. "I should have known I never hit enough to get a headache."

A few more plays. The quarterback throws—complete! A running back says, "This game may be a joke, but I'll tell you what, we're ready. We'll give it our best shot."

But three practices in shorts do not equal a month's work in pads. The game should have been a total mismatch.

Thibodeaux didn't make the practices but he showed up at the game. He had lost weight—most of the alumni had, taking off ten, twenty, even thirty or forty pounds, and looked like normal people. Thibodeaux was ready to play.

Seven thousand people are in the stands. The alumni offense starts the game, gets a first down, then stalls. The defense goes out and soon Nathan Bell, a defensive tackle who was drafted but didn't make it, comes huffing off, winded. Paul Brock, who played defense at Tulane but made the pros as an offensive lineman, is saying, "It's stupid for me to play. I could get hurt. Maybe I'll go in for a down or two. Maybe I won't play at all."

That's fine with the coaches, who want a practice, not a game. Except for some cameo alumni appearances, third-stringers play for the alumni team. The Varsity scores a few times. No one cares. The alums are all clustered around the bench happy to see each other, rehashing old times.

But then on the field one alum makes a great play, smashing a blocker and tackling the ball-carrier for a six-yard loss, and another alum shouts, "All right! All right! Trapani's kicking ass *again*!"

So the alums move to the sideline and start to watch with interest after all, and Nathan Bell goes back into the game and then Brock, what the hell, goes in, too, on goal-line defense. On his first play he is wedged backward and the Varsity quarterback sneaks over to score.

Brock doesn't like it. He stays in, and on a pass play sacks the quarterback. Bell meets him there, and the two of them alternate big plays, penetrating and destroying. Then Alexander and Lapeyre do the job, but Brock is the best, hitting, hitting, intense and punishing. And suddenly an all-alumni, no third-stringers, defensive line hits and hits and hits and the Varsity cannot handle them. The third-stringers pick up on it and play over their heads. Then a first-stringer cheap-shots a third-stringer, and the alumni sideline erupts. Thibodeaux storms the field, is pulled back, shouts, "I got your number! I got your number! I'll get your ass!"

Brock stays in on offense now, Thibodeaux comes in, too, blocking *wham* and the alumni . . . score!

Suddenly this joke has become a game, a real game, and practice be damned. The hitting crackles in the April sun, and both sides are out there for one reason: to win. And in the fourth quarter, there comes a moment when it seems the alumni have a chance to do just that. All they need is one drive and one break, and they have been playing well enough for both. They have taken over the game. And the one coach remaining from when these alumni played sends in an all-alumni offense, untainted by third-stringers. Eight minutes left and it is their game.

But while they are huddling, another coach waves them back to the sideline, and yells, "Student play! Student play!"

As a gimmick to generate interest among undergraduates, the head coach had promised to suit up and play four students. They have nothing to do with the football team, and two of the students are female. They are all sent in. *Not now,* the alumni shout, *not now,* for the play will count. But the boy and girl in alumni uniforms run a pass play against the boy and girl in varsity uniforms. The quarterback throws—intercepted!—and it *counts.*

The alumni have never touched the ball but lost their chance to win.

"Can you believe this shit?" one alumnus snorts in disgust. "Can you believe it?"

Thibodeaux has stopped watching. He is already on his way to the locker room. He had played for two reasons, to see his old teammates and share that closeness once again. And because, no matter what he said, he loved the game. There was still a little kid in him who loved to play. He was walking off before they killed that kid completely.

Five years after that game Thibodeaux was still in New Orleans, doing all right. He had worked as a salesman, got married, and works construction. I talked to the secretary at the Tulane football office the other day. She's been there for eighteen years, through five coaches. "Miz Fitz," everyone calls her. A lot of former players stop in to visit occasionally, especially those in New Orleans. But, she says a little sadly, not Tommy.

REGRETS

I played football in high school and college, coached at four high schools, two as head coach, and two colleges as an assistant, but my own deepest regret from my years in football has nothing to do with losing, or with the game being over. It has to do with a game that one boy never really got a chance to begin.

Oh, I certainly suffered my share of painful losses, two in particular, one as a player, one as a coach, and both by a score of 20–19 in the last seconds. After each one I literally could not eat for several days. But now I think even of them with fondness, for they remind me of the intensity of the moment and players who did and still matter to me.

I remember lining up at what would now be called outside linebacker, us leading 19–13, trying to stop our arch-rival's march down the field at the end of the game, watching them inexorably squeeze out three fourth-down plays by inches, us coming so close and yet failing to stop their progress toward the end zone. And I remember watching the killer extra point. But with even greater vividness I remember tackling a running back on the sideline and knocking down one of their cheerleaders and how when I helped her to her feet she seemed so astonishingly fragile and the day suddenly smelled like fall.

As a coach I remember our scoring on our last drive to take the lead, again by 19–13, missing the extra point but our sideline erupting in celebration anyway with only seconds left. And the other team on the last play threw a desperation pass that our safety—trying to intercept—knocked up into the air. I remember watching the ball, a few feet from where I stood on the sideline, float into their receiver's hands while our safety both fell to the ground and tripped another defender, then watching their receiver jog nonchalantly and invincibly right down our suddenly hushed sideline to score.

But as I said, as much pain as those losses caused at the time, they don't hurt now. Now they bring back to me a time of life.

Only one thing really haunts me from my years in football, and that involves something else entirely. I was coaching just for fun that year, after having coached in college, after having been a head coach in high school, just helping out my own former coach Al Morro, who had become a friend, at Classical in Providence. By then I had found some success as a writer; I had even had some stories published in national magazines.

We played Mt. Pleasant, another Providence school, which had lost more than thirty games in a row. We beat them easily, but they had one terrific football player. He wasn't very big by college standards but he played with as much heart as anyone I had ever seen. On offense he played guard well enough that one of our best defensive players, Ken Thompson, came off the field shaking his head at how hard he hit and at his tenacity. But the kid's real calling was linebacker. He tore up the field blasting through blockers, filling holes, knocking fullbacks backward, chasing down ball-carriers who had broken clear of everyone else. Mt. Pleasant was in our conference and played many teams we also played, so between scouting both them and their opponents I saw four or five of their games, and this kid always played well. He was probably the best football player I saw that year at any position. Despite his size I knew he could play college football.

A week or so after the season ended, the conference coaches got together to pick an All-Conference team and make recommendations for the All-State team. Al hated doing this stuff so he asked me to go. No wonder he hated it. The process in itself was corrupt. Our conference had been allotted a fixed number of All-State positions no matter how many kids, or how few, actually deserved the honor. (Sportswriters don't do any better; I recall one college player who made the Associated Press All-New England team even though he got injured in pre-season and never played a single down.)

I was fully prepared to support—indeed insist on—this Mt. Pleasant kid getting one of the All-State slots even though his team had not won a game. But his coach did not nominate him for All-State, or first string All-Conference, or second string All-Conference, or even honorable mention All-Conference. No one, myself included, was going to push hard for another team's player over his own, so the kid received no honors whatsoever.

I talked to our players about him and learned he was a tough working class kid, Italian. His family had no money; if he was going to go to college at all football would have to take him there. But he had clashed repeatedly with his coach. That wasn't a surprise; his coach had been in charge through four entire seasons without a victory, went through the motions, and was a fool, while this kid cared and went full speed. His coach was not going to help him get a scholarship, and only an extraordinary athlete with objectively measurable talent—a state champion sprinter for example—can get a scholarship without his own coach's support. But this boy had won my heart with his play. To play with his intensity for a winless team and a coach with whom he clashed required almost senseless discipline, commitment, and love of the game. I decided I would help him. I planned to call several college coaches I knew well, men who trusted my judgement, tell them about him, explain the circumstances, and then send the film of our game so they could see for themselves how well the kid played.

I patted myself on the back for my good deed, tracked down the phone numbers of a couple of the college assistant coaches I knew who had switched schools, and dug out the film of our game to mail.

But I never got around to making any of the calls. I never sent the film. I never got around to doing the good deed. A couple of weeks later I headed back to New Orleans, back to writing.

The kid didn't go to college. Now I can't even remember his name.

I've made my share of mistakes, many of them pretty stupid. But there haven't been many times when I had the chance to make the world a little bit fairer, when I knew something was so right, and simply didn't do it, when I had real power over someone's life, if only over a single individual, and failed to use it responsibly.

My failure haunts me in a way that even other failures do not.

WASHINGTON
Wright's Play

Power is a zero-sum game. If one person has more, someone else has less. Usually whoever starts to lose that game, who starts to lose power, will fight before yielding any.

Wright wanted no less than to rearrange the balance of power between the Congress and the president. That was obvious even to outsiders. But to confront a president, he also needed to make the Speakership more powerful within the House. And this was no game.

That meant he needed to take power from committee and subcommittee chairmen—members of his own party, people whose loyalty he needed—if he could. It would be a subtle shift of authority, too subtle for those outside the House to notice. But inside it was noticed.

In the House power was atomized. Political scientist Norman Ornstein has observed that in 1963 only twenty-six House members had press secretaries; within twenty years virtually all 435 did. Although Gingrich was alone in his sophistication about the media, nearly all members knew enough to use it to influence policy and advance more personal agendas. In addition, the number of subcommittees had grown dramatically over the years. By the time Wright became Speaker, well over one hundred subcommittees existed, and each chair tried to exercise tight control over everything within the subcommittee's jurisdiction.

There was also something more basic operating. Wright's colleagues had elected him Speaker, and each was a prince in his or her own right. As Machiavelli warned, "A man who becomes prince with the help of the nobles finds it more difficult to maintain his position than one who does so with the help of the people....He finds himself surrounded by many who believe they are his equals, and because of that he cannot command them the way he wants."

Nonetheless, the Speaker had many procedural weapons at his command to bend colleagues to his will. Tip O'Neill had been a strong Speaker, but under him the House still ran loosely. The nuts and bolts of the place rattled; O'Neill had not turned the screws. Wright intended to turn the screws.

If he did so, he risked sparking a rebellion. He would take that risk.

THE FLOOR

S am Rayburn, the legendary Speaker of the House, used to say that if one could not smell the mood of the House, if one could not walk on the floor and feel it, then one did not belong there. Under Jim Wright—and later under Newt Gingrich—the floor mattered less and less; the leadership, the Rules Committee, and the whip task forces restricted its role. More and more, the floor simply ratified policy. But the floor still mattered. It was controlled largely by procedure, by rules.

Normally the House convened for legislative business at noon on Mondays, Tuesdays, and Wednesdays, and 10:00 A.M. on Thursdays. Committee hearings were held in the mornings, so as not to conflict with floor activity. Thursday the House always convened early so it could finish business in time for members to take early evening flights back to their districts. Friday was usually a brief pro forma session.

In midweek, with the House in session, usually no more than twenty or thirty members could be found on the floor, including a representative of each party's leadership to make sure no one sprung any surprises, along with a bill's floor managers. If the rule for the bill called for two hours of debate, the floor manager for and against the bill each controlled one hour, and doled it out to colleagues in intervals no longer than five minutes. "I yield three minutes to the distinguished gentlewoman from Rhode Island," the manager would say, or, "I yield to my friend the gentleman from Louisiana such time as he may consume."

The floor had a casual feel then. The few members lounged about, sitting together in small clumps in the rows of comfortable tan leather seats, each wider than a first-class airplane seat. One member might have his feet up on the row in front of him. Two or three would be standing in the back of the chamber on the plush blue rug, near the door to the cloakroom, smoking a cigar, leaning against the brass rail behind the last row of seats.

But in every representative's office, TV sets were on monitoring the floor. If something happened, if the bells went off or the circle of small lights which surround every wall-clock in the Capitol lit up indicating a vote, members suddenly interrupted appointments and flocked to the floor. It only took seconds to actually vote, to slip a plastic card the size of driver's license into a slot and push a button. But few members just voted and left. The floor then became a marketplace; members did business, looked up someone with whom they needed to talk. So activity ebbed and flowed; the floor swelled, reaching its peak between fifteen and twenty minutes after a vote started as members flooded it, then contracted as most left. The rhythm of the floor was real and tangible to those sensitive to it; it emanated from the exchanges between members.

One could read those exchanges. There are 440 seats in the chamber. Though none are assigned (unlike the Senate, where each senator has a desk, fixing him in place), certain groups gravitated toward certain seats. Was there someone with one group who did not belong there? If so, what was he doing there? What was Norm Dicks doing with that guy? They hated each other. What were they talking about? It couldn't be arms control, not with them. It had to be the Price-Anderson Act. Yes! Dicks seemed to be making progress. How many votes did that mean? Four? And over there, those members listening to Stenholm, did they seem to be agreeing? noncommittal? Over there, that guttural laugh coming from Murtha—that wasn't the way he laughed at a joke, it meant something else. He was going to stick it to somebody.

Only a few months into Wright's speakership, despite tremendous legislative successes, a discontent pervaded the floor. Members felt they had been working too hard. They seemed already worn out and irritable. They came to the floor and left it impatiently. Their jokes had a harsher edge. Underneath the surface, not showing, were rumblings. One *could* feel it. Wright had already extended his reach far enough to rub up against limits members expected him to respect.

Yet Wright believed he could not let up. He drove so hard. Particularly he used procedure and the Rules Committee to maximize his chances to win. Yet procedure was honor codified. Justice Felix Frankfurter wrote, "The history of liberty has largely been the history of procedural safeguards." Wright was taking more and more procedural safeguards away from the Republicans, walling them off from any say. And Wright pushed hard on every vote. Even Democrats, for all their victories, were restive. They did not like being pushed for votes. The more Wright pushed, the more members were likely to sooner or later say, *Leave me alone for once. Is every Goddam bill a leadership initiative?* Democratic Congressman Marty Russo observed, "If there's a problem with this leadership, it's that they want to win too much."

Wright spent nowhere near the time on the floor his predecessor Tip O'Neill had. Wright didn't like to; members always descended on him with requests, requests that either Foley or Wright's top aide John Mack could take care of. But he knew not being on the floor weakened him.

"I want to spend more time on the floor," he said. "I should. But it's hard to schedule that." *Schedule time for the floor?* O'Neill had lived in his seat in the front of the chamber, or in the cloakroom, and had always known the pulse of the House. Wright risked misreading it. The danger would come over time, the danger that he would grow away from it.

Everywhere Wright turned now he bumped into limits, pushed against them. Every Thursday morning, amid a buffet of coffee, several kinds of juice, fresh fruit, pastries, and bagels, Wright laid out his agenda for the next week to the whip organization, about seventy members—more than one-quarter of all the Democrats in the House. The meetings also gave Wright feedback.

In October, Tom Foley, the majority leader, told one meeting that the next week's schedule included a "labor" bill—an AFL-CIO priority. Members erupted in protest. They hated labor bills because no matter how they voted, with or against unions, they made enemies. A vote that made enemies was a tough vote. Members did not like making enemies. Members particularly did not like making enemies of either organized labor or the business community. *Those people would raise money against you. Hell, they'd even run someone against you.* Wright was bumping into another limit.

Foley told one protester, "Look, labor supported you, raised money for you, set up phone banks for you, gave you volunteers, did everything they could to elect you, and now you don't want to vote on this bill?"

"Right," came back the response.

And if it was bad enough to make enemies, to do it for nothing? Reagan would veto any labor bills. Why force a tough vote when nothing would come of it. Another member jumped to his feet and complained, "I don't know about your state but let me tell you about my state. My two senators go into the AFL-CIO convention and get a standing ovation. Then they walk across the street to the Chamber of Convention and get a standing ovation. *And the reason they can do this is that the Senate is smart enough not to schedule any damn labor bills for a vote!* Why are we scheduling one for a vote?"

Why? Because the leadership had made a deal with labor.

"The house has already passed this bill twice," Foley said. "You've already gotten it on your records. We thought this would be the easiest vote. The Senate will vote this year. Labor knows we're not scheduling any more labor bills unless the Senate passes them."

"*What!?*" a third member hissed from the back of the room. "*Did he say there were going to be more labor bills?*"

The labor bill was not all. Against the advice of his own staff, Wright tried to push the Agriculture Committee to rewrite the Farm Bill, which was supposed to cover four years and had been passed barely a year earlier. And on an appropriation bill, it looked like the leadership would suffer its first defeat.

The bill spent more money than the budget called for. Conservative and moderate Democrats were angry over it. On the floor, they were attacking it relentlessly. A conservative Republican moved to eliminate all foreign aid, which would cut $300 million for Central America both the Reagan White House and Wright badly wanted. It passed. Then a liberal moved to cut $432 million from a farm program, and won a $90 million cut. One region was attacking another, one interest attacking another. The leadership was losing control of the floor.

Members were getting angrier as evening came. Thursday evening. Already members had missed flights back to their district, back home to see their wives and kids. They were stuck here and getting contentious. They went out to dinner and grew almost belligerent. With each vote on each amendment, the mood worsened. It was moving toward midnight. Some members went out for a drink, came back to vote, went out again, came back half-lit and bristling. Claudine Schneider, a moderate Republican, stayed in her office alone, coming to the floor only to vote: "The vibes around this place were too negative."

Florida Democrat Buddy MacKay was proposing an across-the-board spending cut. The leadership could smell defeat. Tony Coelho, the whip, and MacKay talked.

What if MacKay exempted the homeless from cuts? If so, Foley and Coelho would vote for his amendment, guaranteeing passage. MacKay wanted to agree, but he had already told Republican Whip Trent Lott nothing would be exempted. He couldn't go back on his word. Your word was all you had in politics. Colleague after colleague asked him to. He couldn't do it. Then Wright sat down next to him and said that Democrats stood for something, not just dollar signs, and, "packaged with the homeless exemption it's a good amendment."

MacKay was in a bind. He could not spurn the Speaker when the Speaker was coming 90 percent his way. He crossed the floor to tell Lott the homeless would be exempted.

Lott stared at him. *That wasn't the deal we made.* Lott had expected to win this, the first win for Republicans all year. Now it was slipping away. They were losing both the political issue—if Democrats voted with MacKay they could not be accused of breaking the budget—and a victory over Wright.

"You're peeing on my leg, aren't you?" Lott snapped.

"But I'm looking you in the eye while I'm doing it."

Wright had prevented an embarrassment, but the House floor was becoming slippery. The House itself was trying to work its will even as Wright was trying to impose his upon it. Everywhere he was pressing, pushing, and he was doing it to a body that had not been pressed or pushed before. His agenda demanded all his time, all his energy, all his focus. And he was getting tired. He *was* tired.

Then came more pressure. Hard feelings or not, a few days later the budget was moving forward. Only the floor vote remained. There were two problems: George Miller and Charlie Stenholm, the party's liberal and conservative extremes. If both factions voted "no" the budget would lose. Word came back that Miller would vote "no" but would not work to kill it, would not try to convince others to vote against it. That left Stenholm.

To Stenholm, the budget was a lie. It claimed savings that were phony.

"Stenholm's not the only one with that problem," one member said at a whip task force meeting to pass the budget. These task forces, anywhere from half a dozen to thirty members, were made up of members who would talk to colleagues both to find out their position and to convince them to support the leadership. "There's no question there are phony savings in here. It's the only thing the Senate would accept."

"Send Marvin Leath to talk to Stenholm."

"Don't send Marvin," warned Buddy MacKay. "He'll tell him the truth."

Suddenly Tim Penny, who with MacKay co-chaired an ad hoc caucus of moderate Democrats, got up and walked out of the room. It was a fact not lost on those remaining. Penny wasn't going to work for passage and might even vote "no." The room grew tense.

Coelho turned to one member and demanded, "You're listed as a 'no response.' Are you with us?"

"Hell, he's sitting right here," said another member. "Of course he's for it."

"You've got to ask a direct question," Coelho snapped. That was the only way to count. Anything other than a definite "yes" was not a commitment. "You can't let him laugh it off. Are you okay?"

"I'm a 'yes.'"

They ran down the list of members to talk to, each member at the table taking some. There would be three more votes that day, so colleagues would be on the floor at least three times. They could whip them then. The meeting broke up and Coelho stepped outside for a moment, then came back in. Five members were still sitting at the table. Coelho asked, "Why aren't you out working?"

"We're trying to figure out what to tell 'em. When the truth's precluded, what other arguments do we have?"

This shift in the balance of power toward Wright—not just away from individual members of the House and Senate but away from the White House as well—created volatility. Power is always accompanied by tension; even when it seems to lie quiet, that quiet comes from a dynamic equilibrium, like the stillness of the rope in a tug of war.

Yet Wright didn't let up. Instead he stretched his power to bring together Otis Bowen, Secretary of Health and Human Services, John

Dingell, Chairman of Energy and Commerce, and Commerce health sub-committee chairman Henry Waxman, along with Appropriations subcommittee chairman William Natcher. Wright was plunging deep inside the administration, directly, ignoring the White House, to decide adminis-tration policy—in this case to plan a program against AIDS. Bowen was willing to cooperate. A former governor of Indiana, he understood power and recognized that the meeting could serve his purposes as well.

"What do you want?" Bowen asked. "A recommendation on how to spend $400 million more than the White House asked for?"

"Yes," Dingell said, adding, "and don't clear it through OMB."

"Could you write me a letter asking for this?" Bowen had to protect himself.

"Certainly," William Natcher, the relevant Appropriations subcommittee chairman, assured him. "I'll send it today."

"Will I have to take the money from elsewhere in HHS?"

Natcher shook his head. "Not if the legislation is drafted correctly."

Everyone smiled. They all understood each other.

Soon Wright pushed against the Constitution itself. The Fairness Doctrine required broadcasters to give equal time to differing political opin-ions. It had been in force for decades, but the GOP-dominated Federal Communications Commission had revoked it. Democrats feared that, without the doctrine, the usually-conservative owners of radio stations could attack them nonstop. Congress had passed a bill writing the Fairness Doctrine into law. Reagan had vetoed it. Congress lacked the votes to override it, so House Democrats stuck it in the Continuing Resolution, a massive bill to fund the entire government.

It was a bill that Reagan had to sign or close down the government. It was a power play. Could Reagan close down the government over some-thing called "fairness"?

But Wright's power play also amounted to overriding a veto without the needed two-thirds vote, raising constitutional questions and infuriat-ing Republicans. It was one more indication of Democrats', and Wright's, willingness to use power.

The House didn't feel right. One could walk down the corridors, walk onto the floor, and sense uneasiness, restiveness, even anger. It wasn't anything one could isolate and say, *There!* But members seemed more into themselves; on the elevators they nodded at one another instead of talking. They came to the floor for votes and left quickly, instead of lingering. There was less mixing in the chamber of Republicans and Democrats. Dick Cheney had always enjoyed talking with Foley on the floor, but had not talked to him since a particularly bitter vote.

More problems were brewing over unrelated Rules Committee restrictions on amendments. Seventy-nine Democrats wrote Wright a letter complaining about the arbitrary silencing of debate. *Seventy-nine!* Yes, the moderates and conservatives from the South had signed the letter. But so had Mike Lowry, one of the leading liberals. And Pat Williams had signed. Williams was one of the members personally closest and most loyal to Wright. People like that signing a protest letter to the Speaker? *Something wasn't right.* The whole feel of the House was wrong, sour, distasteful.

Another Democrat complained, "Wright doesn't let these guys play. He's got his fucking agenda. That's it. The leadership's got to understand, these guys have to play. In a democracy you should be allowed amendments on the floor. If someone ever decided to fuck Wright he's in trouble. There's so much unrest it's unbelievable."

PEACE

There was no respite. Nor was there time or opportunity to wait for one, not unless Wright was willing to let go, to let his agenda escape. Instead, Wright made himself more of a target both inside and outside the House.

The most emotional issue of the time, the single issue that penetrated to the gut, was the civil war in Nicaragua. Most Republicans considered the "contras" both freedom fighters and a bulwark against the spread of revolution in Central and South America. So the Reagan administration felt justified in supporting in every way possible—including breaking the law—the contras in their guerrilla war against the Sandinistas, avowed Marxists who ran the country.

Most Democrats considered the contras murderers, operating illegally. Funding them made Congress complicit in murder.

Simple arithmetic showed the Reagan administration that it lacked the votes in Congress to continue to fund the war.

What would become an extraordinary exercise of power by Wright began on July 22, 1987—by coincidence the day after Gingrich first demanded that Common Cause's Wertheimer call for an Ethics Committee investigation of Wright—when Tom Loeffler had approached Wright with an idea. Loeffler was a senior White House aide and former GOP congressman whom Wright trusted. His idea: Wright and Reagan would endorse a joint peace plan for Nicaragua. Its bipartisan nature, Loeffler argued, would put enormous pressure on the Sandinistas to accept it, ending the war.

Contra opponents, including the overwhelming majority of the House Democrats, believed the whole plan was a trap. Several times in the past, the Reagan administration had announced diplomatic initiatives and then abandoned them after Congress approved money for military assistance. Most Democrats believed that the Reagan administration would do the same thing again, only this time their own Speaker was playing the fool for them; they expected the White House would make certain that the Sandinistas rejected the proposal. As David Bonior warned Wright, "I think the initiative will fail and they'll be able to say, 'Look, we tried the Speaker's plan, it went nowhere, now give us the military aid,' and they'll have the votes."

Loeffler may well have been sincere, but Bonior accurately described how Reagan's State Department and National Security Council saw the issue. House Republicans saw it that way too. In one meeting with several Democrats Trent Lott blurted out, "We're not without risk if it entails pulling our punches. Then the trap will have trapped us."

The trap will have trapped us.

But Wright sensed another possibility—peace. Loeffler had walked into his office fifteen days before a summit meeting of five Central American presidents was to convene to discuss a peace proposal advanced by Oscar Arias, president of Costa Rica.

After Loeffler's first visit, Wright, an expert on the region, personally contacted several Central American heads of state and their most senior advisers, as well as the Nicaraguan ambassador. Each one assured him that a bipartisan proposal coming from the United States might well lead to a peace agreement. So Wright pushed to finish the joint proposal with Reagan before the Central American presidents met. Indeed, he dictated the bulk of it, and it was modified in a string of intense discussions with Secretary of State George Shultz and congressional leaders of both parties.

The day of the Central American summit, August 5, the White House publicly released the plan agreed to by Wright and Reagan. Arias asked Wright to send a representative to the talks; Wright sent Richard Pena, who had no time to pack so much as a change of underwear for his trip into tropical summer heat. Wright sent a message with him: "Tell my friends Duarte [Napoleón Duarte, president of El Salvador] and Arias that we are not dictating anything to them. We want to offer all the support we can."

But the administration was using the media to direct the course of events. At 7:30 in the morning, while Wright was appearing on *Good*

Morning, America to explain the peace proposal, Loeffler called Wright's aide John Mack to apologize for newspaper stories and explain they were having some difficulties getting everyone in line. Mack nervously looked at the papers. *They're screwing us,* he thought.

The whole point of the peace plan was to develop a bipartisan policy that had credibility, that did not seem a ploy. What gave the peace plan international credibility, and credibility in the eyes of the Sandinistas, was Wright's involvement. The significance and the symbolism of the Speaker of the House of one party joining with the president of the United States of another could not be overstated. State Department, House, and Senate historians all agreed: no member of Congress had been so prominently involved in foreign policy since Henry Clay, before the War of 1812.

So those in the administration who wanted the peace plan to fail hoped to get the Sandinistas to reject the peace overture by convincing them that it was a political ploy designed to get more contra aid. They downplayed Wright's role. They found a ready audience in the press, and particularly in the *New York Times.* The *Times* was the most respected and powerful paper in the country, and probably in the world. Readers believed it. Readers around the world believed it.

Thursday's *Times,* August 7, 1987, was filled with coverage, including two stories by White House reporters, the lead page one news story by Steve Roberts and a "news analysis" by Joel Brinkley.

No contra supporter could have hoped for more than the *Times*'s analysis. Nowhere in the story did Wright's name appear, nor was there a single reference to the meeting of the five Central American presidents— the meeting which Wright had hoped so much to influence and which was occurring that very day. Brinkley's opening sentence read, "As it has before, the Reagan Administration offered a Central American peace plan today in the full expectation that Nicaragua would reject it, several Administration officials said." He concluded that the plan was strictly a ploy and also stated, "The Central American states also were caught unaware, State Department officials said." Yet Wright had talked directly with heads of state of those Central American countries. Brinkley's story was not only flawed in its analysis, it included flatly untrue information.

In Steven Roberts's twenty-nine-paragraph front page news story, Wright's name appeared first in paragraph twenty-three. The first sentence of the story announced the agreement. The second sentence read, "But many Democrats expressed concern that they were being deceived and that the plan, discussed with Congressional leaders on Tuesday, was primarily a public relations tactic." The third sentence of the story read, "Some administration officials said the plan was offered in the full expectation that Nicaragua would reject it. The reasoning, they said, was that such a rejection would assure approval of renewed aid to the contras later this year by demonstrating the insincerity of the Sandinistas."

Roberts's story was all true, but only part of the truth. It reflected several institutional problems of the White House press corps. What most White House reporters know best is politics, and they naturally emphasize what they know best. Also, to make a story interesting for a viewer or reader, they often personalize it. Therefore, their reporting tends to focus on terms of who's-on-top, where's-the-political-advantage.

That tendency is compounded by the impossibility of one reporter having independent knowledge of more than a few policy areas. Yet White House reporters must cover whatever issue the White House chooses to emphasize on a given day—be it arms control, criminal justice, housing, tax policy, or anything else. That ignorance makes White House reporters easier to manipulate, particularly since they need information instantly and therefore must rely on White House sources. In a speech to political scientists, Roberts himself recognized this factor: "At the White House, the odds favor the sources of news, not the reporters. The power of officials to dole out or withhold information is sizeable; returning or not returning phone calls is the ultimate leverage. But on Capitol Hill, the advantage shifts to the journalist. Sources are everywhere. The people who try to dissemble or prevaricate lose their credibility and get left behind."

In the case of the Central American peace proposal, the media's natural inclination to emphasize political gamesmanship was fed by sources whose purpose was served by encouraging that view. Even a senior White House official conceded, "I think [Elliot] Abrams's people at State and the National Security Council people were the ones trying to kill this, particularly José Sorzano."

Sorzano, a Cuban refugee, would not return telephone calls from reporters who knew Central America well, like *Newsday*'s Roy Gutman, author of a book on the region. Gutman knew too much, knew all about the planned summit. But Sorzano talked to the White House press corp anonymously. The press has to be willing to grant anonymity to get in-

formation. Anonymous sources are especially important—but also especially dangerous and manipulative—when contradicting a public position. The *Times* reporters were used. The power of the *Times* magnified
the impact. The anonymous attacks on the policy were a way affecting
that policy. They threatened the chances for peace.

In this case events moved too quickly for the media to play much of a
role. Wright's personal conversations with the Central Americans had
assured them that even if the administration was not sincere he could
control congressional funding. And the Sandinistas also could see this
was their best chance of ending a war that was as deadly to Nicaragua as
the American Civil War had been to the United States.

Less than twenty-four hours after the *Times* stories appeared, at 4:30
the next morning the phone woke Wright at home. The call came from
Guatemala. He quickly focused. The caller explained that President Arias
had asked him to call, certain that the Speaker would not mind being
awakened for this news. The five Central American presidents had set-
tled their differences and, God willing, would sign a peace agreement later
that day. They had reached a peace agreement. President Arias wanted
to thank him for his support and to tell him that without the stimulus
provided by the initiative Wright had co-sponsored with Reagan, the
agreement would not have been possible.

Wright closed his eyes and said a short prayer. A calm spread through
him as deep as anything he had ever known. *Blessed be the peacemakers.*

Wright's daily press conference began at 9:40 A.M. It was only eighteen days after Loeffler first had walked into Wright's office. A reporter
opened the press conference asking, "Mr. Speaker, do you have a time
for the debt ceiling vote?"

"I will let Tom Foley tell you about what is going on there. Let me
give you a little bit of news that I think is very good news. I got a phone
call at 4:30 this morning.... Ambassador Fernandez said the five countries have accepted the Arias plan for peace in Central America with certain modifications and variations embracing some of the things that we
had recommended."

Reporters sprinted from the room to check with the State Department.
State denied that an agreement had been reached. Then a State Department official called Wright's office to ask, Where did the Speaker get
these ideas?

State's ignorance of the agreement reflected its entire approach to the region: for years it had pressured, even bullied, the Central Americans to support the contras. Central Americans had resented this. Earlier in the year, Arias had been infuriated at what he regarded as slights during a visit to Washington. As a result, the State Department lacked solid information. Assistant Secretary of State Edward Fox later conceded, "We were completely surprised by the peace agreement."

Later that afternoon, Wright taped the Democrats' response to Reagan's weekly five-minute radio address and closed: "May we all ask the blessings of God on their endeavor."

Just then an aide walked in with a wire story out of Guatemala. The five presidents had signed the agreement.

"By God," Wright said. "That's great."

THE VOTE

The constitution gave the president control over foreign policy. Outside the House, Republicans were furious over Wright's dominance of Central American policy in defiance of the White House, which still wanted military aid for the contras despite the peace agreement.

Inside the House, Wright was engendering even greater fury. The Speaker leads the entire House, not simply a party, and is charged with insuring fairness in all parliamentary procedure. Shortly before Wright became Speaker, Gingrich noted, "You don't mind losing if you've got a clean vote. If he gives us that, he'll take a lot of the poison out of this place."

Instead, Wright had exploited every advantage he could extract from the rules to advance his own and his party's agenda. The poison built. And he was about to push even harder. He was about to shake the institution.

Days before, the stock market had registered its greatest percentage loss in history, a one-day 508 point drop in the Dow—equivalent to a 2,200 point one-day loss in the year 2001, and nearly twice the percentage loss of Black Tuesday in October 1929. And that 508-point drop was only the single biggest loss in a string of record losses.

In the wake of the market collapse, the entire American economy seemed briefly to teeter. There was concern that, as in 1929, the market would drag it down. The most important thing Washington could do was bring down the deficit, which had skyrocketed. When Reagan entered office the national debt—all the debt the nation had accumulated in more than 200 years—was $930 billion; when he left office it would be more than $2.6 trillion. In just eight years, then, the debt of the preceding 200 years almost tripled. Market observers believed that concern over the debt and interest rates caused the market collapse.

Congress had passed a law requiring that the deficit be cut by a minimum of $23 billion. But there was no agreement over how to reach that total. The market collapse forced the White House and Congressional Democrats into a budget summit to reach a compromise.

Wright believed that the correct economic policy was to both cut spending and raise taxes, to demonstrate to the markets that Washington was serious about deficit reduction. He wanted to pass a bill that would do that and use it as the basis from which to negotiate with the White House over the budget.

But there was an additional wrinkle. Dan Rostenkowski, chairman of the Ways and Means Committee, had gotten a major $5-billion welfare reform bill through his committee. He did not have the votes to pass the bill on the House floor. So he asked Wright for a favor—a big one. And it involved abusing procedural power.

In each Congress, the two most partisan votes are the first two: the first elects the Speaker and the second adopts a set of standing rules. Each party offers a nominee for Speaker and a package of standing rules, and the winner will govern the House for two years. For example, according to the Democrat-written rules for the 100th Congress under Wright, although Democrats had only a 59 percent to 41 percent advantage over Republicans in the House, Democrats held a two-thirds plus one advantage, nine Democrats to four Republicans, on the Rules Committee. (In the 107th Congress, elected in the year 2000, Republicans held a 51 percent to 49 percent advantage over Democrats, but also had a nine to four advantage on Rules.) And since 1974, the Speaker has appointed all of his party's representatives on Rules.

The Rules Committee matters because it writes a specific rule covering how every piece of major legislation is handled on the floor. This rule dictates which different parts of a package, if any, will be voted on separately, what amendments can be offered, how long it shall be debated, and so forth. On the floor, the House (the Senate, which operates under standing rules, has no comparable procedure) first debates and votes on the rule for a bill, and only later on the bill itself.

In procedure lies power.

Process. Suppose there are two bills. One is very, very popular; the other is unpopular. Suppose the Speaker had the Rules Committee link the two bills together and only allow members one vote—they either pass both bills or reject both bills. The unpopular bill passes. *Process.* The Constitution stipulates that the House and Senate will write their own rules; that means that House rules take precedence over the law, possibly even over the Constitution itself. Suppose a law—the law of the land, approved by the House and Senate, signed by the President— required the House to allow a vote on a certain issue. Suppose the Speaker asked the Rules Committee to write a House rule that voided the law. *The rule takes precedence over the law.*

The rule is supposed to govern only procedural issues. Procedure is the prerogative of the majority. Members of the majority routinely vote for a rule which guarantees a bill's passage, then vote against the bill itself. Their vote for the rule simply affirms that their party controls the House. The public doesn't understand the complexities of procedure—it's too hard for an election opponent to explain.

Rostenkowski asked Wright to include a $5-billion welfare reform bill as part of the rule, including substance in what should have been only a procedural vote. Rostenkowski's bill could not pass on its own. For complex reasons of internal House politics, Wright agreed. If the House passed the rule, then it would automatically pass welfare reform—without any debate over the issue, or any chance to amend it. The unfairness inflamed every Republican in the House, and many Democrats. So did the welfare reform bill itself, which was far more liberal than the House wanted. A groundswell of rebellion began to develop, led by Texas Democratic Congressman Charles Stenholm.

The vote on this procedure would be one of two defining events in Jim Wright's speakership.

Wright expected half a dozen members at the meeting. Stenholm arrived with twenty-five. One after another they trooped into Wright's office, southerners and moderates and even some liberals, filling the chairs and couches and standing, crowding in on Wright. A leadership aide stood in the back of the room and took down names. They had Wright's attention all right.

Stenholm spoke first. He applauded Wright's statement that $23 billion was only a start in deficit-cutting, then suggested dropping welfare reform, keeping the taxes, and cutting spending $2 for every $1 in tax increases. Stenholm wanted to be allowed to offer an amendment calling for his package.

"That's difficult," Wright replied. "The DSG has a [liberal] substitute they want to offer. I can't say 'yes' to one, 'no' to another."

"So what," said another member. Let the House work its will. "Why not let Charlie and the DSG both offer amendments?"

"Give us votes," Stenholm urged. "Give us alternatives. Otherwise we all will do what we have to do."

"What's important," said a third, "is welfare reform. If it comes out, I'll vote for the bill and work for it. I can't vote for it if it's in there."

Half a dozen others seconded him. Wright urged them to vote for the bill regardless. It was crucial for the country.

The meeting ended without resolution. Stenholm stood up and said, "If welfare's in there, it will lose."

The pressure on Washington increased. All day the stock market slid lower and lower. In 1929, after the initial crash a series of smaller quakes had sent the market down far lower still. Was this happening now? In New York, in Washington, in every city in the country, fear of a real collapse underpinned every conversation. Former President Gerald Ford called Reagan, Wright, Bush, Dole, and Byrd from New York with the same message: the markets needed an agreement quickly, and it had to include taxes.

Wright made calls to colleagues looking for votes while Foley met with lobbyists from over forty organizations and pressed them to lobby for passage. They left fired up, eager to work.

Wright also made an assessment: Stenholm said his plan included Social Security cuts. If that was so, Wright could simply beat it on the floor. He offered Stenholm a deal: he could offer his amendment if he would vote for the rule, against the GOP substitute, and for final passage of the main bill. It was dangerous. If Stenholm dropped Social Security cuts from his proposal it could pass. "We don't want to tell him you can't offer it because we might not be able to beat you," one member worried. But they needed his vote. Stenholm said he was considering the deal and would get back.

This was a tough vote. Freshmen Democrats in particular were worried. Most had won tough races and the first reelection campaign was always the most difficult. The whip count listed most as undecided. Twenty freshmen gathered to hear from the Speaker, the majority leader, and the whip.

When Wright entered, the freshmen rose. It was odd, this show of respect, members of Congress—princes in their own right—standing for him. More senior members would never have done it. He smiled in appreciation and began to talk softly, so softly they leaned forward to hear, speaking not of politics, or of favors, but simply of the merits of the bill, the reasons why the economy needed the tax bill. Welfare reform, too, was a good bill. And so it would be included as part of the rule for the larger bill. "You can nit-pick any bill to death. You can always find an excuse to vote 'no.' But Felix Rohatyn, Gerald Ford, half a dozen other people have been talking to me about the need for taxes as part of the package. None of them have mentioned welfare. Tax and spend is better than borrow and spend, borrow and spend, borrow and spend. It's the constitutional responsibility of the House to move a tax bill first. That is our institutional responsiblity. And if we can't vote for this tax bill, what can we vote for? It's a good bill."

His voice was still soft, soft but insistent, soft but piercing, soft but dogged, dogged, dogged. Then he stiffened, bunched his fists, and his voice, though still soft, tightened. "If we pass this, then we're strong. If not, then we have no position. The markets will read that as a terrible message, and they will be right. This is the most important vote of the year." He closed simply, saying, "Do this if you can."

He left. Foley took over and made it simple, an issue of power. He talked about the rule, and procedure. "It's a question of who's running this House."

Then Tony Coelho, the whip. Coelho was the first whip elected by members; before him the whip had been appointed by the Speaker. He had his own power base and his own agenda. Coelho leaned hard on the freshmen, harder than Foley, harder than Wright. "You came here to govern," he told them. "Nobody said it was easy. I know what you really want. You want to vote 'no' and have the bill pass. Look me in the eye and say that's not true. You look me in the eye and tell me that."

Coelho's intensity had a physical feel, like a man pushing his face forward, making others withdraw. He did not let them escape. Then he asked, "Are you with us?"

The pressure seemed to pay off. Only three of the twenty freshmen said they would vote "no," and one of those three said he would vote "yes" on the rule.

But the pressure was on. It wasn't the best way to count. Counting votes resembles gathering intelligence; it should be done coolly, without pressure. Whipping is delicate, trying to convince while simultaneously trying to get an accurate count. Here members were saying "yes" when they wanted to say "no." Coelho had always counted so accurately. In his election as whip he had asked his own campaign manager point blank for his commitment. How solid was a commitment given at the point of a gun?

"You can't bully people," Jack Brooks, one of the toughest members of the House, once observed. "You never want to ask someone to do something they're really against, or that hurts them in their district. They're the sole judge. The test is not whether someone votes with you, but whether they tell the truth about it. If you say straight out you're not for it, well, I can't fault you. I know where you are. That's your business. Flexing muscle is foolishness. Even Lyndon Johnson said you have to be careful not to unintentionally hurt someone."

At the next whip task force meeting, even task force members raised objections to the rule. Why force a tough vote on this?

"With the climate in the country we can't afford not to pass it," Coelho argued. "We can't afford to wait. If we have the votes on the rule there's no reason to allow any more votes—" no amendments.

If we have the votes on the rule there's no reason to allow any more votes. To Coelho the floor was a place to ratify policy, not to make it. Other members viewed the House as a deliberative body, a town meeting; they saw the floor as the place deliberations occurred. The more limitations placed on the floor, the more members were cut out of policy-making. The Democratic Caucus was willing to accept some manipulation of procedure for reasons of convenience—it allowed them to get home at a reasonable hour, and it protected them from tough votes—and power. It allowed Wright to exercise power as its surrogate. But it wanted Wright to recognize limits. That wasn't because of sympathy for Republicans. On the few occasions Republicans had controlled procedure in 1981, they had pioneered exactly the things they later decried as abuses of power when Democrats did them. And on the very first procedural vote of this year, Republicans had taken what then Republican Whip Dick Cheney conceded was "a political cheapshot at the Democrats"—and an infringement on free speech—by making it against the rules to discuss raising income taxes on the House floor. So Republicans hardly had clean hands. But Democratic members wanted the leadership to recognize limits.

And Coelho didn't have the votes. Only 173 members had said "yes," with 20 a firm "no." If the leadership lost 20 more Democrats out of the 65 undecided, they would lose.

That evening Wright sat down with his top aide John Mack. The door was closed. No one would open this door, with him in with Mack. They reviewed the names of members who had a problem with the bill. Wright looked at name after name. "These are good people," he said. "We can't lose these people and win."

"Those freshmen aren't so sure either, when you ask them one on one, out of the group."

Wright pointed at one name.

"You'll never get her. Fear. You can see it in her eyes."

"That's the trouble with this place," Wright snapped. "Too many people here who shouldn't be in Congress. No guts. That's what leadership is. If you don't have it, you shouldn't be in government." He looked over the count. "We're at the point we should be picking up votes. We're not. I'm uneasy. This is too big a vote to be uneasy on."

Wright had decided. Welfare was almost certainly coming out. He picked up the phone and called Stenholm.

"Charlie, how are you?" The massaging began. The leaning began. Pressure? What's pressure? Barney Frank had said, "There's nothing higher than the Speaker asking for your help. There's nothing higher than that."

"Charlie, I had planned to have you offer your substitute.... They're not with you on that?" Stenholm couldn't get enough people to support raising taxes and cutting Social Security to make it worth putting on the floor. He didn't want to offer it now—it would only show how weak the position was, which would undermine any chance of the budget summit doing something big. Wright continued.

"Charlie, I value your information. If we took welfare out, do you think it would pass?...I think you're real important Charlie, I think you're key....Could I have your help?...It certainly matters for me."

All those times back in the early 1980s, Wright would sit down next to Stenholm on the floor, argue for a vote, and Stenholm would shake his head and say, "Jim, I just can't do it." Wright had taken it personally, had wondered about his own ability if he could not even convince a junior colleague from his own state, but he had never asked on a personal basis. Now he would. That was the one thing higher than the Speaker asking for help. Asking on a personal basis.

Wright listened for a moment, then dropped all pretense and made himself vulnerable, in a way naked. Members did not expose themselves like that. "I never put it to you quite this way before Charlie. If this doesn't pass, my name is mud. I said we're going to do it. My name would be mud, my reputation zero. They'd say, 'Hell, he can't even deliver the House....' Appropriations? You better believe it, buddy. That language is in there.... I want $23 billion just for starters. I'm committed to doing more....Not your vote, Charlie. I want your help...." He had it. "Thanks! Thanks a lot, buddy!"

They hadn't made a deal. Stenholm's support remained contingent upon welfare coming out of the bill, and Wright had not promised to remove it. He had kept the "if" in his request. Still, Wright had all but announced it would come out. Stenholm expected it out, and, with it out, he had agreed to work for the bill. Stenholm *was* key. *Not your vote, Charlie. I want your help.* With Stenholm working actively for the bill, passage became certain. There was something else. Wright had made it personal. Stenholm had said yes.

That could become a bridge to Stenholm for the future, a healing of old wounds on both sides. Stenholm had his resentments, too. That healing would begin out of mutual self-interest, but it might build upon that, into trust and respect and a positive desire to work together wherever possible. If that happened, Wright's base within the Caucus would become more solid than his predecessor O'Neill's had ever been, and in many ways—in useful ways, in ways which allowed things to get done—more solid than Rayburn's. At that moment, as Wright hung up after talking with Stenholm, Wright's speakership seemed capable of achieving the greatness and permanence he had dreamed of.

The next morning Wright sat down with Coelho and Foley. The count was only up to 187. And they were still counting the rule. Who the hell knew how many were willing to bend to the pressure on the rule but vote against the bill? Wright wanted welfare out.

Coelho fought the decision. "We need twenty-eight more to pass the rule, counting absences. I see thirty-four, without even using the big gun—you."

"Wait a second, Tony," Wright replied. "There are guys on here saying 'no' we don't lose often. We've got a chance of losing this bill. Stenholm and Leath will try to help, if we take welfare out."

"I don't believe that. People are 'no' because of taxes. They're using welfare as an excuse. Stenholm's a 'no' on taxes."

"Stenholm's problem isn't taxes. The same with others. The count hasn't moved in twenty-four hours. That makes me nervous."

Coelho countered, "The Black Caucus is saying if welfare comes out they're 'no.' You lose as many as you gain."

That was news. A major factor. A very major factor. Wright and Foley were unhappily silent for a moment, absorbing the information.

They would run one more whip count, then decide. Foley and Coelho left. Wright picked up the phone and started making phone calls in alphabetical order. The first one was to AuCoin. He had a long way to go.

At 12:30 the leadership met again. The count looked better—up to 213. In addition, five members had said they would help if absolutely necessary: they swore that their vote would not defeat Wright.

"What about final passage?" Foley asked. "People who say 'yes' on the rule, 'no' on the bill? We can lose the rule, and that's not a disaster. Losing final passage is a disaster."

"We should get seven to ten Republicans on final passage,"Coelho predicted. They returned to the list of swing votes. Coelho picked out a name. "It's taxes with him."

Foley and Wright both disagreed. "Tony, he told both of us with welfare out, he'd vote for it and work for it. He can't back up on that."

They had ten more votes if welfare came out. But if the Black Caucus did walk, that balanced out. "I don't like welfare in the bill," Wright grumbled. "It shouldn't have been in there in the first place. A damn power play by Rostenkowski."

"If we get 218," Foley said, "let's go for it."

Wright had to make a decision. In or out?

What was the decision? Wright looked straight at Coelho. It was Coelho's job to count. Wright thought back to the day just before summer recess when Coelho walked into his office and said that Wright wasn't treating him properly. That he was not being respected. Now Coelho was saying they had the votes, and that taking welfare out would lose votes in the Black Caucus. If Wright disagreed, it would be the ultimate statement of no confidence.

Welfare reform stayed in.

Outside, in the Speaker's Lobby, standing on the carpet thick with history, Mack worried. "I've done a thousand vote counts in the last eight years. Winning ones and losing ones. I always knew where we were. I don't know on this one." He looked through the swinging doors to the House floor, looked at it as if it were a strange and dangerous jungle, and fell silent, then added, "There's a different feeling out there."

The whip task force was finally working on passage of the bill itself. At long last it had finished counting the rule. Both would be voted on the next day. Wright rarely attended a task force meeting. He walked in. Marty Russo, the chairman, said, "The rule's up to 217 now, from 187 yesterday. Your presence was felt, Mr. Speaker. Thank you."

Wright nodded but was still uneasy, and huddled with an Arkansas member who then picked up the phone to call Bill Clinton, then governor of Arkansas and head of a bipartisan governors' welfare reform group. Could Clinton call Arkansas members? And send telegrams to everyone else? Yes.

Russo read off a name. One whip reported, "The stuff the Republicans are throwing out about the bill cost us his vote."

"It was the *Wall Street Journal* story this morning, about all the goodies in the bill for some people," said someone.

Ways and Means Republicans had leaked a list of tax breaks Rostenkowski used to buy votes. The *Journal* had trumpeted them. Wright, with a venom that expressed his feelings toward the press, spat, "People wrap the garbage in newspapers."

Things weren't supposed to go this way. Losing votes at this stage. Now was when votes started flocking to you if you had any momentum.

Outside in the corridor, Chief Deputy Whip David Bonior snorted, "There's so much shit in this bill—$100 million for big chicken farmers like Perdue. Rostenkowski's in this pissing contest with Harold Washington [the black mayor of Chicago, at war with the white political powers] over some municipal thing. If we do win the rule, final passage is not at all assured."

Then word spread across the floor about money an Appropriations subcommittee had just given the Pentagon. When Russo heard of it he was furious. He believed that the number violated a pledge Wright had made to him earlier.

Stenholm was angry now, too, angry with a deep personal anger. Wright had asked him for help on a personal basis. He had said "yes" on a personal basis, as long as welfare came out. He had gone around telling his colleagues welfare was out. It wasn't. Wright had made a fool of him, embarrassed him. Beyond that, he had thought after Wright's call that maybe they could work together in the future, maybe there was a softening of the hardness between them. He had hung up with a good feeling. But welfare was in the bill. Wright had made it personal and then decided he hadn't needed him and spurned him. Well it was personal now all right.

Thursday morning, the morning of the vote, the vote count looked all right on paper. But the House was seething. The regular weekly whip meeting in H-324 seethed with seventy Democratic members present. The Democratic Caucus, for the first time all year, began to splinter. There were so many agendas, so many ambitions, so many beliefs. The leadership was accommodating itself to one of them only: to Rostenkowski.

Liberals exploded over the money for defense. And defense wasn't even in the bill about to be voted on. It had nothing to do with the bill. As members shouted at each other, Wright tried to regain control.

"Defense is next week's problem. You have a commitment from us for savings on that. Please. Please, let's talk about this week's game."

"We'll turn this into a task force," Coelho announced. "Final passage. If you're in the whip organization you're supposed to work."

It was an arrogant and patronizing remark. They were all equals, all princes. They did not take orders, least of all from Coelho. Most of the whips walked out.

Coelho and the leadership staff ran down a handful of names. How about this guy?

"He's okay. I had his biggest fund-raiser call him last night."

"No he's not. He's wrong on the rule, right on final passage. That's Stenholm. Stenholm's working hard."

"He told me 'yes.'"

"That was before Stenholm talked to him."

"Christ. If Stenholm's making ground up we don't even know about...."

The vote on the rule would come at noon. Members flooded the floor for a quorum call at 11:30; organizations from both sides worked the members hard.

Democrats were exercising pure power, Republicans were playing pure politics. By law, the deficit had to be cut at least $23 billion. The Democratic proposal did that. The GOP proposal did not. The GOP plan cut the deficit only $15 billion. Despite the greatest stock market crash in history, despite the law, despite demands from around the country for cutting the deficit by at least $23 billion, House Republicans chose to fall more than one-third short of the goal. They did so because they could not make enough spending cuts to reach the target and would not include any tax increases at all.

Partisanship fed on itself, drove each side apart. Faced with the irresponsibility of the minority, the majority grew contemptuous of it, more determined to govern in spite of it, and more arbitrary; faced with the increasing arbitrariness of the majority, the minority grew more irresponsible and more destructive of the institution.

While the debate proceeded, members worked the floor. Dingell talked to Buddy Roemer in one part of the chamber while Stenholm hung back. When Dingell left, Stenholm moved in. Then Stenholm with another member, and another. Stenholm ally Tim Penny with his list of names worked them, shaking a hand. Got him! Of all the House, less than a dozen members would decide the issue, all of them Democrats. Two members and a Foley aide talked to Les Aucoin. Wright talked to AuCoin. Got him!

Wright stood in the well of the House, the pit of the amphitheater. The chamber was full as he closed debate for his side. As he spoke, shouts of VOTE! rang out in the hall. VOTE! The time for talking was over. *VOTE!*

Wright continued. "We have been marching up this hill all year, knowing we had to face this choice sooner or later.... That Constitution which we have been at pains to honor this year very plainly and unequivocally says that all revenue measures must originate in the House...." VOTE! "If you are serious about deficit reduction, this is your chance. Vote 'aye' on the resolution, 'aye' on the rule, 'aye' on the bill."

The vote on the rule started. The leadership fell behind almost immediately by ten votes, then fifteen. Slowly the Democratic leadership climbed back up, down twelve, down eight, down four, down two. But the mood of the House was running against them. No Republicans voted with them. Thirty-five Democrats voted "no." Thirty-seven. Forty. *Forty-one!* A loud cheer went up from Republicans! Forty-one Democrats, combined with all the Republicans, meant an absolute majority. Then forty-three, forty-four, forty-five. Democrats who had promised to support the leadership if their votes would make the difference had started voting "no." Ultimately, forty-eight Democrats voted "no."

The final result: 203 in favor, 217 opposed.

Wright had been beaten! The Democratic juggernaut had been stopped.

The chamber was strangely still and Republican leader Bob Michel rose and addressed the chair. "Mr. Speaker. Under somewhat otherwise normal conditions, noting our unanimous vote on this side, we would be elated with this victory. Mr. Speaker, we do not look upon it that way.... It has been my feeling that men of good will might bring their divergent thoughts together.... I for one am grateful for the vote defeating the rule, but we are not gloating over it.... I would hope that it would signal our intention ... to work together hand and glove in a bipartisan way to come to a final resolution."

Wright, on the floor, rose to respond. "I appreciate what my friend the gentleman from Illinois has suggested. He has been consistent, suggesting all along that we delay, and see if we can get some signal as to what the president will accept before we try to pass anything. If we do that, it puts the total initiative in the hands of the executive branch of government over something that the Constitution declared was the primary business of the House of Representatives. I bow to the majority. The majority quite obviously did not want this particular rule . . . [with] a welfare reform bill. . . . Therefore, the Rules Committee will meet at 12:45 and we will be seeking another rule."

Trent Lott, the numer two Republican in the House, rose. "What does this now mean? This matter cannot be brought up again today. . . . Are we going to be in session tomorrow to continue this effort?"

The standing rules of the House stated that if the rule for a bill was defeated, another rule could not be brought to the floor the same day. Only a two-thirds vote—an impossibility—could suspend the standing rules and waive that requirement.

Foley answered him: "As I understand what the gentleman has just told me, it is most unlikely we will be given authority to proceed with a rule filed on the same day. Under those circumstances, it is my duty to inform the House that not only will there be roll-calls this afternoon, but the House will come in at 10:00 tomorrow and will stay in session until we finish the bill."

This fight had only begun.

For Wright, it was as if all the detritus had been cleared away, all the excuses, all the complications. What was left was pure action. It was what he loved.

"Okay. What did we lose by?"

"Fourteen. We need a change of eight."

Wright named one member. "He said he was with us on the rule and voted 'no.' Get him in here. There are fifteen members who told me personally they would vote for the bill if welfare came out. Put together a meeting of all the moderates we can get, down in 201." A member on the Rules Committee asked what he wanted in the rule, and Wright ordered, "I want it clean."

Foley, Coelho, and Mack each picked up one of the telephones scattered around the room. Wright went over names. They were going to win this thing dammit. They were going forward and would win it.

A few minutes later, Wright returned to his personal office and called Gus Hawkins, head of the Black Caucus. Hawkins said he didn't care if welfare came out of the bill. He hadn't cared if it was in in the first place. Wright's jaw tightened. Bill Gray and Charlie Rangel, also members of the Black Caucus, also confirmed that the Black Caucus didn't care. That wasn't the information Coelho had given Wright.

Then Mack suggested something. A few years earlier, Tip O'Neill had lost a rule. It had been a minor fight, and for convenience he had formally adjourned the House and then convened it again immediately. That had created for parliamentary purposes a new legislative day. The parliamentarian had ruled the action permissible. Then O'Neill had brought a new rule onto the floor.

Wright could do the same thing. They did not have to wait until tomorrow. They could bring the rule back this afternoon. There were two reasons to do so. First was convenience; members had made plans to be home tonight and in their districts tomorrow. Now they would have to cancel their appearances and stay in Washington. Second was politics. Overnight the GOP might gain momentum; the next day's papers would trumpet Wright's defeat and might lock that defeat in. But if they voted today and won, the story would be his victory. The defeat would be forgotten.

There was one reason not to do what Mack suggested.

It would violate the spirit of the House rules.

Did Wright want to go forward?

It was a defining moment. Everything, all year, had pointed to this bill. But that was policy. Honorable men could disagree on policy. Wright prided himself on fairness, talked of his love for the institution and his responsibility to protect and represent it. Procedure was honor codified. Wright wanted this bill passed. The Constitution required that revenue measures begin in the House. To do anything else, even to enter these budget talks, without a bill was to compromise the integrity of the House. Or was it just ego? Just willfulness? Just wanting to win? Wright was determined to act. He was caught up in his passions and it was his nature. They would do what Mack suggested.

Everything for the rest of the 100th Congress, everything for as long as Jim Wright would remain Speaker of the House, flowed from Wright's decision.

The decision was not totally arbitrary. If Republicans agreed, there was no problem. Foley checked with Michel. Their conversation was brief. Foley later said, "He sort of grunted. There was no indication it would spark a strong reaction. If I had gotten one, I'd have gone back and argued the case."

Everything else was moving on schedule—the phone calls, the meetings, the strategy. He met with one group of members after another, liberals, Ways and Means members, and the Black Caucus. Votes began to shift. At one meeting, though, George Miller complained about the extra $3 billion in defense spending which would be voted on the following week. Wright offered to give him an amendment to strike it.

"Mr. Speaker," Miller said, "I don't say this as a threat. I'm not going to let you down. But I don't want an amendment. It would lose. I want you to cut the $3 billion."

"I can't give you that commitment right now. But maybe you have a point."

Wright had done what there was to be done. He went to lunch in the members' dining room and sat there calm and certain. Action calmed him. The fight calmed him. His favorite poem, which he learned as a small child and knew by heart, was Kipling's "If." *If you can keep your head when all about you/ Are losing theirs and blaming it on you./ If you can trust yourself when all men doubt you,/ But make allowance for their doubting too.* Action itself was his element. And he was acting. Someone asked him why he had left welfare reform in the rule, why he had overruled his own instincts. A hard edge came into his voice: "Because I trusted my vote counters. I trusted people who told me things that weren't true. Maybe I won't trust them so much anymore."

Coelho was his vote counter but he never mentioned his name, nor did he ever raise the issue with him. A few days later Wright invited Coelho to join him on a trip to Costa Rica over Thanksgiving and to the Holy Land for Christmas. He observed, "You have to work with people as they are, not as you wish them to be."

It was time to go back to the floor.

While Wright was eating lunch, the whip task force to pass the bill met. Marty Russo didn't attend. Russo had considered himself chairman of the welfare reform task force, not the tax bill task force; welfare was gone now, and so was he.

Like Miller, he was angry over the $3 billion extra defense had gotten. That afternoon he played basketball in the House gym. Going for rebounds his elbows whipped through the air, sharp elbows flying; playing defense he put his body on people. When anyone said anything—anything—to him he flared up. A colleague thought, *What the hell's wrong with Russo?*

It was twenty minutes to three. Foley took the floor and moved that "pursuant to clause 4 of rule XVI, that when the House adjourns today it adjourn to meet at 3:15 today."

The implications were not lost on Republicans. They erupted suddenly in disbelief and outrage. Wright was violating every pretense of fairness.

Ed Madigan, the chief deputy GOP whip from Illinois, his words masking his rage, asked, "Do I understand the purpose of our having two legislative days in one calendar day is so that the House avoids the necessity of having a two-thirds majority to be able to consider this? So what we are doing is just to further diminish whatever role the minority is entitled to play in the deliberations of the assembly, is that correct?"

Foley tried to calm the Republicans, saying it was strictly a convenience to allow members to keep appointments in the district for Friday. But there was no calming the Republicans. The floor hissed with emotion, constrained by formal decorum.

Conservative Republican Robert Walker said, "I wonder if the gentleman understands why we would be a little upset.... I would say to the gentleman from Washington, I mean we are being terribly abused and this is an outrage in the way the House is being conducted—" Democrats on the floor interrupted with sarcastic groans—"Well you can all moan but I will tell you this is a terrible injustice. For a party that says it stands for fairness and justice you all are abandoning any pretenses of it on the floor today."

William Dannemyer, another conservative Republican, said, "Genesis tells us that the Lord created the world in seven days. We are now witnessing the creation of an eight day. I just ask the gentleman, does he have a name for this new creation?"

"Yes," replied Foley. "It is called the Guaranteed Deficit Reduction Act."

The House adjourned at 3:05.

At 3:15 it reconvened, with all the accoutrements of a new session including a new prayer by the chaplain, and the announcement by Wright
with which he opened every session, that "the Chair has examined the
journal of the last day's proceedings and announces to the House his approval thereof."

Angry Republicans demanded a vote on approving the journal. Walker
rose again. "Parliamentary inquiry, Mr. Speaker? We are about to cast a
vote. Is the journal available for inspection by the members?"

"The journal is indeed available," Wright said evenly.

"Yes," chortled a Democrat. "In shorthand."

Inexorably, the Democratic machine marched forward. At 4:45 in the
afternoon, the House approved the new rule, once again on a party line
vote, once again voting on control of the House, with even Stenholm
voting with his party.

But the next vote was on the bill itself. At last things had reduced
themselves to the simplest point.

The debate went forward on the floor while Wright worked the phone,
worked one member after another. "Who the hell am I calling?" he
asked at one point an instant before saying, "Hey, how are you?" while
an aide wrote down the name and shoved it in front of him. It was an
Oklahoma member. Wright told him his colleagues in two adjoining
districts were now voting "yes," protecting him, and asked, "Do you
have any specific personal problem?" But the man had made a campaign
pledge to vote against taxes; no favor Wright could do could outweigh
that.

Wright got a report that Bill Richardson wanted something personal
all right; to chair the platform committee at the Democratic National
Convention. Wright, the convention chairman, fumed, "I'm not giving
that away. A fellow has to understand you don't vote against something
like this and get that."

Another man in the room suggested, "You don't have to promise. You
don't have to say it. Have Mack say it. A staffer. That's no commitment."

Wright shook his head no. He wouldn't mislead him. But he could go
at Richardson another way: "Tell him you heard a member say that that
SOB can't ask for something like that if he votes 'no' here."

The leadership tried a new ploy: asking members who were going to vote "no" to not vote at all. It might be an easier sell than a "yes" vote. But it was also the most delicate of all requests. Asking members not to vote was asking them to violate their most solemn responsiblity. Wright didn't want to ask that. He didn't want to ask that. Others asked for him.

At 7:05 in the evening, debate ended. It was time to vote on Michel's substitute. It lost 229 to 182, while Wright went from member to member, checking most closely with those who had told him they would not let the bill lose—they would vote with him if they had to. He pulled Jim Chapman aside, a junior congressman from Texas who had won election only because of Wright's direct personal involvement. Chapman assured him, his would not be the vote to beat the bill.

Wright climbed the steps from the floor to the Speaker's chair. "The question is on the passage of the bill," he announced.

The first vote was by voice and pro forma—no one would accept its result—yet both sides shouted loudly.

"In the opinion of the chair," Wright announced, "the 'ayes' have it."

"Mr. Speaker! On that I demand the 'yeas' and 'nays'!"

As with every roll-call vote, the panels behind the press gallery, above and behind the Speaker's Rostrum, receded and the wall became a gigantic tote-board with each member's name lit up; a red light beside it would indicate a "no" vote, green, "yes." On either side of the chamber, a clock began counting down from 15:00 to zero while also noting the vote totals. The leadership clustered around the computer terminals—each party had two, one in the front of the chamber, one in the rear—which would show vote break-downs by party, region, state. The Republicans started ahead, Democrats pulled even at 158 each, then fell behind 158–162, then pulled ahead 172–168. Wright seemed in control. Democrat Nick Rahall from West Virginia, who disliked what the bill did to coal, was surrounded by six members, and three literally had their arm on him. *All right Goddammit.* He voted "yes." Four members wanted new committee assignments and had had discussions earlier with Coelho, who made no absolute promises—not even Wright could absolutely guarantee a committee assignment—but he pledged leadership support. Each voted "yes."

Things looked good for Wright. Suddenly a red light went up by Chapman's name. Chapman had voted "no." Members surrounded him now. What was going on? What was wrong? Wright talked to him. Nothing was wrong, Chapman said, it was just that it looked like they wouldn't need his vote after all, so he had voted "no." If they needed him, he'd switch.

Meanwhile, George Miller and Fortney "Pete" Stark, two California liberals, walked into the men's room off the Speaker's Lobby. Once, when Wright was sixty, Stark, who was erratic and who was a generation younger, called him a "cocksucker." Colleagues stepped between them. Wright invited Stark outside. Stark wouldn't go. Wright then sent word that unless Stark apologized, the next time Wright saw him, wherever that was—including on the floor of the House—he would knock him down. Stark apologized. Stark was a subcommittee chair on the Ways and Means Committee. This was a Ways and Means bill. Members of all committees, much less Ways and Means subcommittee chairmen, supported their committee's product.

Miller was emotional. He had ridden over in the subway thinking he would vote "yes." But that $3 billion in extra defense spending gnawed at him. It gnawed at him. That afternoon he had told Wright, "I'm not going to let you down." Suddenly Miller thought, *What am I? A horse's ass?* Earlier Wright had promised the Pentagon wouldn't get that much. Wright was making a fool of him. Suddenly tense, almost in tears, he walked onto the floor, shoved his voting card into the slot, and punched the button for "no."

Across the chamber, John Mack saw him come in, looked up at the board, saw the red light next to his name. "George!" Mack shouted. Miller walked out. Mack shouted, "Mr. Foley! Miller just voted 'no'!" Foley ran after him, racing to catch Miller before the elevator arrived, caught him, and said, "We're going to lose this thing."

"Tom, I'm just so goddam mad, just stay away from me."

"I just thought your vote was a mistake."

"I can't help you."

Foley watched him step onto the elevator. A moment later, Mack looked up at Stark's name. *Stark voted "no." Goddamn that son of a bitch.*

On the other side of the chamber, Marty Russo came in. He was furious over the defense spending figure, too. From Chicago and on Ways and Means, he and Rostenkowski were almost like father and son, so this was his bill too. But Russo walked in, voted, and went straight to the airport. It was 7:30 now. There was an 8:00 flight to Chicago. Russo voted "no." A Wright supporter ran up to Rostenkowski and jammed his finger into Rostenkowski's chest. "Your man fucked us!" he shouted. "Your man!"

From the other side of the chamber Bob Michel saw the commotion, looked up at the board and saw Russo's vote, and thought, *We're going to win this thing.*

Wright was on the floor trying to find in the swirl of 435 members those who had promised to help if needed.

The clock stood at 0:00. The time on the clock didn't matter. The rules said a minimum of fifteen minutes were required, but the vote stayed open as long the Speaker wanted. The vote could stay open forever. The vote stood 201 for the bill, 202 opposed—where the hell was Chapman?— then 201 to 204.

If it was a tie, the Speaker could vote. Where was Chapman? Now it was 202 to 204, 203 to 204, as those members who had promised not to let Wright lose voted "yes." 204 to 204. *Thank God! The Speaker could save the bill!* But suddenly the other side came up with two votes—204 to 206. Then it was 205 to 206. 205 to 206. 205 to 206. *Where the hell was Chapman? Why wasn't he on the floor?* 205 to 206.

"Chapman's in the cloakroom!"

Coelho ran in after him. At first he could not find him. Not by the phone booths, not in the chairs, not by the hot-dog stand. In the far end, in an area darkened so members could lie on a couch and sleep, was Chapman. Coelho said they needed him. Chapman shook his head. He wasn't coming out.

Outside in the chamber the vote remained 205 to 206. Republicans were exuberant, the chamber raucous. A Republican shouted, "Regular order!" It quickly became a refrain. "ORDER!" "REGULAR ORDER!" Make the vote final.

"REGULAR ORDER! REGULAR ORDER!" The chorus of Republicans in the chamber grew louder and louder.

Coelho and Chapman argued, then Coelho came out and found Mack. "He's not coming out!" Coelho hissed. "He gave the commitment to the Speaker, not to me. You go in after him."

A leadership aide ran up to the chair and told Wright that Russo was on his way back from the airport, hold the vote for Russo. Bonior, as if to confirm it, held up one finger and shouted, "ONE MORE!" It was a routine announcement, telling the chair to hold the vote open for someone hurrying to the chamber. Bonior was playing for time. Jim Moody echoed, "ONE MORE!"

Trent Lott ran across the chamber, out into the corridor, out onto the great stairway that leads to the plaza, then returned and shouted to the chamber at large, not to the chair, "There is no one out there, no one in sight!"

Regular order! Regular order! REGULAR ORDER!

The clock ticked. Mack was in the cloakroom, leaning on Chapman, leaning on him, leaning on him, not with threats but with *You owe it to him. You can't let this happen to him. Everything he's done for you, you've got to do this for him.* Democrat Mike Lowry ran to the front of the chamber playing for time: "Mr. Speaker, how am I recorded?"

Bonior echoed him. "Mr. Speaker, how am I recorded?" Then Martin Frost. Then Bill Ford.

The parliamentarian whispered to Wright. Wright announced, "The chair will announce that there is no procedure for members to ask how they are recorded. They may look and see. The chair has been advised that there were other members en route to the chamber."

He stood above the floor, alone atop the rostrum, alone, speaking into that hushed wildness. With each passing second his reputation for integrity dissipated. He felt the eyes of the entire chamber on him. Finally he announced, "If there are no other members who desire to vote or to change their vote, all time has expired."

The Republicans cheered! They had broken the machine. This victory! This massive victory! They had broken the machine! Bonior yelled—just to delay—he wanted to change his vote from "yes" to "no" and asked for the red card which members used to do so. But bursting down the aisle from the back door, desperate, charging—*hold the vote!*—came John Mack. Behind him was Chapman. Wright saw them, leaned forward to Bonior, and said, "Take back that damn red card."

Bonior looked up. Chapman asked for a green card, to change his vote from "no" to "yes." The House was in an uproar.

As Chapman switched his vote, Wright's voice rang out—never varying throughout the count in inflection, always even—"If there are no other members in the chamber who desire to vote—" *BOOOO! BOOOO!* rang out in the hall, an extraordinary outburst for the House of Representatives, shouts of *BUSH LEAGUE! BUSH LEAGUE!*, a raw, almost murderous anger unleashed, Lott so furious he slammed his fist against the solid wood lectern before him and shattered it—"or if there are no other members who desire to change their vote, on this vote the "yeas" are 206—"

"Mr. Speaker, I have a parliamentary inquiry!" shouted Gingrich. It was the only way to stop the announcement of the result. Madigan, a member of the GOP leadership, assuming Wright would win had skipped the vote and gone to the Kennedy Center. Was he on the way back? How long until he arrived? But they needed two votes, since one would create a tie which Wright would break. One Republican, Jim Jeffords, who was running for a Senate seat in Vermont, had voted with the Democrats. *Where was he?* (In 2001 he left the GOP, changing Senate control.)

"The gentleman will state it."

"Mr. Speaker, I would inquire of the parliamentarian and the chair, once the Speaker has said the vote is closed and all time has expired, and we have that on the tape, on the video tape, once that has been done how can that be reopened?"

"The chair will state that it always has been the disposition of the chair and of every occupant of which the present occupant is aware to permit any member who is in the chamber to vote or change his vote so long as he desires to do so. The chair had been advised that there were other members en route and therefore the chair was holding open, and still holds open, if members wish to change their votes or other members wish to vote. . . . If no other members desire to vote or to change their vote, the yeas are 206, the nays are 205."

Mickey Edwards was on his feet—every member was on his feet— "Mr. Speaker! I have a parliamentary inquiry!"

"The gentleman will state his parliamentary inquiry. If it is a parliamentary inquiry the chair will entertain it."

"I do have a parliamentary inquiry. I would say the Speaker did not answer the last one. After the chair has said, 'All time has expired,' which the chair did, can you then reopen the vote?"

Under the rules of the House, Wright's having said "all time is expired" meant nothing; what made the result final was saying "the bill is passed" or "the bill is defeated."

"The chair will respond. On more than one occasion, the present occupant of the chair and in the chair's observation other occupants have permitted members to vote so long as these members are in the chamber and obviously desiring to cast a vote."

"Further parliamentary inquiry!" Edwards said.

"The chair will ask—" Wright now ignoring Edwards—"if any member desires to vote or to change his vote? And if not all time has expired. The yeas are 206, the nays are 205. The bill is passed."

The bill is passed. *BUSH LEAGUE! BOOOO! BUSH LEAGUE! BOOO! BUSH LEAGUE!*

It was ugly, the ugliest any member living had ever seen the House.

Wright finally broke free of the press in the Speaker's Lobby and returned to his office. At times during the year he had been tired. Even weary. But that tiredness had always been physical. He was sixty-four years old but vital, with a well of energy, still pounding a punching bag that hung in his home. Suddenly he seemed old, like old men one sees on the street whose bodies have shrunk, whose clothes hung limp, who have become less than they once were. It was as if the fight had gone out of him, and the pride and force with which he naturally carried himself had disappeared, and so his clothes hung limp now, his whole body sagging. In his office, he smiled weakly. "I was holding the vote open for Russo. Someone told me he was coming back. I was holding it for Russo. Not Chapman. . . . It didn't help my reputation. To have people impugn my integrity—" He shook his head sadly—"to have Republicans shouting like that."

Then he fell silent.

He was a man who had dreamed of greatness and largeness for himself and greatness and largeness for his institution. A House like Rayburn's House, a House where colleagues respected each other, where Rayburn and Republican leader Joe Martin had loved each other, yes loved each other, where when Martin was defeated for reelection as Republican leader by Charles Halleck, the man to whom Martin fled was Rayburn, his old dear friend Rayburn.

This vote had destroyed Wright's vision of the House. Reduced him now to partisanship, narrowness, divisiveness. It wasn't what he had wanted. It was the opposite of what he had wanted. He ached. A friend reminded him of Rayburn's similar moment in the chair shortly before World War II, when while votes shifted back and forth he had abruptly declared the vote final. His action had preserved the draft by a one-vote margin.

Wright shrugged off all consolation and sat alone with his thoughts.

Meanwhile, Republican leader Bob Michel was standing in the corridor outside his suite of offices. They were better really than Wright's, in the old part of the Capitol, elegant marble and tile on the floors, oriental splendor in the ceiling frescoes, and much more space in Michel's personal office than in Wright's. It had been the Speaker's office, but Rayburn and Joe Martin had alternated between Speaker and minority leader, and the last time Democrats took control, in Wright's freshman term and two years before Michel's election, Rayburn had suggested to Martin they just stay where they were instead of moving. The Republican leader had kept those rooms ever since.

Now Michel was telling a reporter Wright's action was "outrageous." The reporter left. Michel seemed now more saddened than angry and said, "Here's something that shows the way this place really operates. My fellows tell me I ought to be outraged."

Then he sighed. He wasn't outraged. He was saddened. Standing there with his hands stuck in his pockets, he seemed like what he was, a grown-up version of an All American boy who got excited over baseball, to whom expressions like "Aw shucks" and "dadgum" came naturally. Wright had courage, extraordinary political courage, and will, and led. Wright had the capacity to make history, to change things. Michel wasn't that kind of leader. *The key to leadership is to listen,* he had said. But he had misread his membership that very afternoon and had not protested when Foley told him of the second legislative day. He had compromised his own policy beliefs that afternoon, too: he recognized that taxes were necessary, had proposed them to Wright, and yet had excluded them from the GOP proposal and fell 35 percent short of meeting the deficit-cutting target. He had made no effort to stop the political games his GOP colleagues played. "There are some things you have to do to keep control," one man close to him said, justifying it.

Yet Michel still had something so solid about him, solid through and through. If Wright was in pain, so was Michel. Michel had the same vision as Wright, of a House warm with collegiality and bipartisanship. Gingrich had consciously tried to destroy that comity because they believed it had led to accommodations which had kept Republicans out of power for all of Michel's thirty-two years in the House.

Thinking of the future, the long-term future, Michel said, "He just doesn't have any give. He just doesn't have any give."

The Capitol had the permanence of stone and yet lived. The great columns, the classic Acropolis-like front, reached backward into the beginnings of democracy. In the early morning light, the Capitol was like some ancient cathedral, with its multicolored tiled floors merging into curved, sweeping ceilings with warm-toned frescoes. In Statuary Hall, the original House chamber, was a statue of Lady Liberty and one of Clio, the muse of history, watching and taking note. Now in the bowels of the building, down the spiraling staircases marked by rough stone blocks, life proceeded: the kitchens baking food, the carpenters repairing furniture, immune and immured to the world of power above them.

The Capitol continued as it always had, but Wright's speakership had changed. The vote had changed it. Wright had stripped power bare and exposed truths, uncomfortable truths. Members shied away from that nakedness. They wanted to avert their eyes, like people who did not want to see cripples, or dwarfs, or amputees, or those who bore terrible scars, in the hope that not looking would make them disappear. The truth was not just that the leadership would strong-arm people, but that some members were cowards.

Wright had called Bill Richardson three times the day of the vote. Richardson, who had offered to trade his vote to chair for a powerful position at the Democratic National Convention, never called back. The next week he told Wright, "I'd have voted with you if I had just known how much you cared about it."

Sure, my friend. Wright smiled that smile of iron teeth and said, "Well, I'm disappointed in you."

The leadership made no apologies. Bonior said, "A lot of people around this place are naive about the use of power. We're not playing a game. For everyone who thought it was a Pyrhhic victory, two people thought it was good. They liked it. It proved we could be tough when we had to be."

Coelho, when asked about Republican reactions, said, "My only response is, what difference does it make what the Republicans think? The only significant question is whether it hurt Wright and the leadership in the Caucus and the answer is 'no.'"

But Coelho was wrong on both counts. The action had ripped open wounds that would have difficulty healing, even within the Caucus.

Republicans mattered too. They would see to it that they mattered. Wright was not the first Speaker to exercise power. Republican Thomas Reed, one of the great Speakers in history, earned the epithet "Czar" for his use of the rules. "Gentlemen," Reed told Democrats, "I am about to perpetrate the following outrage," and once said, "The right of a minority is to draw its salaries, and its function is to make a quorum." Dick Cheney, the heir-apparent to Michel (Lott, fed up with the House, had decided to run for the Senate), had written a book in which he had praised Reed, and Wright quoted it to reporters.

But Cheney was outraged. And Cheney was a bellwether. Although conservative, he had always distanced himself from Gingrich and believed that the minority had a responsiblity to participate in the legislative process rather than use it to create political issues. He was solid, respected, trustworthy, but he also was one of the few members of the House who could compete with Gingrich intellectually, and who was wholly comfortable with ideas.

Earlier, he had been pleased by Wright's fairness in handling such issues as the Iran-contra investigation and had said he had "a good professional relationship" with Wright. Now he told a reporter, "This was the most arrogant, heavy-handed abuse of power I've ever seen in the ten years that I've been here. You have a Speaker who's perceived by Republicans and Democrats alike as a guy who can run the place, not because he's respected but because he's a heavy-handed son of a bitch and he doesn't know any other way of operating, and he will do anything he can to win at any price, including ignoring the rules, bending rules, writing rules, denying the House the opportunity to work its will. It brings disrespect to the House itself. There's no sense of comity left. Why should you, if you are a Republican, and given the way Republicans are treated, think of a Democrat as a colleague? They aren't colleagues." To another writer he said, "Wright told us Republican votes don't count as much as Democratic votes."

Tip O'Neill had always let the House work its will. Wright had bent it to his.

The feeling among Republicans was clear: *Do anything. Get him.* If opportunities did not arise, they would create some. Gingrich would create some. Gingrich had already publicly compared Wright to Mussolini. If Wright could bend the rules for his own purposes, why couldn't others break unwritten rules for their purposes? Wright would deserve anything he got. Members who had ignored Gingrich, disdained him even, now paid him attention. With regret Cheney now said, "That vote's made Gingrich a big man in the Republican Conference."

The House at night, in the cold of winter, is itself an image of power. Lights shining on the Capitol make the white marble luminescent. The great white dome atop Capitol Hill is visible for miles. One stands close to the buildings and feels the cold radiating from the immense, thick sandstone columns. One stands there and feels the chill, the chill of power. Great large blocks of stone and marble, cool even in summer. Yet the building, so lit up that it has the homey feel of a Christmas tree, is always alive, always with people about, as vibrant as Times Square, but different from there too. Here everyone—cops, chaplain, staff, members— know everyone. It is as impersonal as history, and yet it is home.

Wright needed peace. Events swirled and eddied around him, threatened him, threatened his power. Gorbachev arrived for his summit with Reagan. At the White House state dinner, Dobrynin told Wright that if the United States complied with the Central American peace agreement, the Soviets would withdraw all heavy weapons from Nicaragua, down to the level of police pistols. Wright raised the question with Gorbachev the next day; he confirmed that he would speak to Reagan about Nicaragua. Wright sent a memo to Shultz asking him to pursue it. Peace. That's what he wanted. Peace.

For Christmas he was planning a trip to the Holy Land with his wife Betty and several members. Christmas and peace. He called one member to invite him and his wife. The member declined. He wanted to be with his kids.

Wright looked out the window for an instant, this man who wanted so much to root himself in time, tracing backwards to find his lost Irish ancestors, and forward, to leave a mark in history that those in the future would remember.

History? snorted a less ambitious member. *You hope what you do matters to someone, helps someone, but this history stuff is crap. Who will remember any of this in fifteen years, much less one hundred and fifty? History is your children.*

Wright tried to make peace. A Republican amendment on minor legislation was ahead by one vote. Wright's vote would defeat it. He refrained from voting, and then waded into the Republican side of the chamber, territory where Wright almost never went, and told the sponsor he had purposely let it pass. It was a humbling thing for him to do, an admission of error, an apology. But Republicans derided his gesture; among them he seemed a modern-day Richard III, abandoned and desolate and surrounded by enemies.

If Wright wanted peace, he would not find it. Not even two weeks after that bitter House vote, Wright would inflame Republicans again. The issue was the contras. The Reagan administration and most Republicans had never embraced the peace agreement reached in Central America. Ever since it had been signed, Wright had engaged in a constant battle with the administration over implementing it. Wright had intervened constantly. Republicans had accused him of setting up a virtual shadow State Department in violation of the Constitution, which reserves the conduct of foreign policy to the administration. Conservatives began to, literally, despise him.

Then, beginning November 11, 1987—Veterans' Day—Wright met three days in a row with Nicaraguan President Danny Ortega. Ortega tried to convince Wright to act as a go-between between the Sandinistas and the contras in their negotiations. Wright refused, and refused to send a representative to those talks. But on Friday the 13th of November he met a third time with Ortega, Cardinal Miguel Obando y Bravo, and papal nuncio Pio Laghi. The Sandinistas had earlier told him that Obando—a long-time critic of the Sandinistas and friend of the contras—was "unacceptable" as an intermediary. But Wright's intent was to convince Obando to accept the role of go-between and catalyst in the negotiations.

Secretary of State George Shultz had asked Wright not to participate in that meeting. Shultz had asked him to leave it to the Central Americans. But the Central Americans—not just Ortega, but representatives of the pro-contra Catholic Church and the Guatemalan and Costa Rican governments as well—were asking him to stay involved. For Wright to proceed was a large thing. Two weeks earlier, *Congressional Quarterly* had run a lengthy story entitled "New Contra Politics: Wright the Dominant Force." That marked a major shift of institutional power. Central America was one of the administration's two main foreign policy priorities—the other being arms control—yet Jim Wright, a Congressman, dominated it. The delicacy of his position, of the Speaker of the House dominating a foreign policy priority of a White House, did not escape Wright; neither did it stop him.

The administration claimed it supported the peace process. But if he withdrew, peace would be in the hands of those who had devoted themselves to funding the contras—even when that meant violating the law.

He saw Obando and convinced him to take charge of the negotiations. Ortega had to accept him. The negotiations later bore fruit. Ultimately the Sandinistas held free elections, lost, and gave up power peacefully. But that came later. Too late for Wright.

Republicans in the White House, the State Department, and the Congress condemned Wright, grunted with disdain at the "Wright-Ortega" plan. Commentators on the Sunday interview shows attacked him too. Then Monday, on his way to defend himself on *Good Morning, America,* Wright read a *Washington Post* editorial accusing him of an "intervention into the day-to-day running of foreign policy that was breathtaking in its scope and whose like is hard to recall.... He overreaches recklessly.... Our misgivings do not center now on the substance but on the procedure. Mr. Wright appears to have gone way over the line that separates opposition from interference."

Coming only three weeks after the most bitter House vote in decades, Wright had touched a nerve. Even Bob Michel was outraged, privately storming at Wright. And Gingrich said, "You cannot overestimate the importance of anti-Communism in the Republican Party. The symbolism of Wright meeting with Ortega on Armistice Day, Veterans' Day, just shook people over here. I think it bothered Cheney more than [the vote]."

Cheney, the former White House chief of staff, deeply believed in the prerogatives of the executive branch. "Jim Wright has radicalized House Republicans," he said.

They set up a task force chaired by Cheney which studied ways to respond to Wright's control of the House. Cheney decided, he said, "to attack targets of opportunity, fight a guerrilla war." His first move: to leak the minority report of the House Iran-contra Committee in advance of the release of the committee report to make sure GOP views got good play in the press. "I wouldn't have done that except for the reconciliation vote," he said. Cheney knew how to play the game. He could be hard, too, although he stayed within the rules for now. Gingrich was operating the true guerrilla war. There was the feeling, spreading among House Republicans and conservatives, that Wright had to be stopped.

WASHINGTON
Gingrich's Play

W hile Wright dealt with the inside game and policy, Gingrich continued his focus on the outside game, the media. It was his only way of achieving power. Even if he wanted to fight inside the House, he didn't have the votes. And he didn't want to. He preferred the path through the media, and through Wright. Earlier he had said, "Wright's a useful keystone to a much bigger structure. I'll just keep pounding and pounding on his ethics. There comes a point where it comes together and the media takes off on it, or it dies."

Gingrich's efforts provide a classic study of how to use the media to achieve one's goals. Wright's response provides a study of what not to do.

THE OUTSIDE GAME

While Wright was infuriating Republicans inside and outside the House by his manipulation of parliamentary procedure and his involvement in Central America, Gingrich sought to influence the media both indirectly and directly. He tried to sell his theme of corruption to people like Norman Ornstein, a congressional expert often quoted by the media; if these experts echoed Gingrich's own criticisms it would help his cause immensely. He also contacted such press heavyweights as the editor-in-chief of *Time*, editors of CBS's *Sixty Minutes*, ABC's Ted Koppel.

For example, to Ben Bradlee, editor of the *Washington Post*, he complained that the *Post* had missed a major story on House corruption, particularly on Banking Chairman Fernand St. Germain. The Ethics Committee had conducted a lax investigation of him—Johnnie Cochran, friend of the chairman, was hired to do it—but even so had concluded that St. Germain had violated both federal law and House rules on his financial disclosure forms, understating holdings by millions of dollars. His staff had pressured regulators to grant favors to a savings and loan in which he was an investor. He had become a multimillionaire through dealings with people who benefitted from programs under his jurisdiction. He violated limits on gifts from lobbyists. Yet the committee recommended no disciplinary action against him whatsoever. On St. Germain, Gingrich was absolutely correct: the Ethics Committee's failure to discipline St. Germain was an outrage and did signify corruption of power in the Lord Acton sense.

And with Bradlee he scored a hit. Bradlee replied, "Dear Newt, You are right. How's that for an upfront confession of error? ... The *Wall Street Journal* owns that story. Despite my heroic efforts, the *Post* reporters are very reluctant to swing in after someone else has broken a story. We should go after it, and we will." Bradlee and soon thereafter *Post* editorial page editor and *Newsweek* columnist Meg Greenfield were among those who received Gingrich's file of negative stories on Wright.

Every major media figure receives dozens of packets every day from people wanting them to publicize their cause. Gingrich's packet was only one of many. But Gingrich was more persistent. What he said was more disturbing. And he was a member of Congress, an articulate and highly intelligent one.

Wright also gave him something new to work with. A month after the initial peace agreement in Central America, *Washington Post* reporter Chuck Babcock, perhaps the best investigative reporter in Washington, broke a major story.

Babcock started working on his story independent of Gingrich, although after Gingrich had complained to Bradlee. Babcock closely examined Wright's involvement with savings and loan executives and decided nothing there was worth reporting; Wright had not acted improperly. Instead, his story focused on a book Wright had written when he was majority leader called *Reflections of a Public Man.* When Babcock asked Wright's staff detailed questions about it, they stiffened, refused to allow him to interview Wright, and required him to submit written questions. His story grew tougher. The facts were tough enough. Wright had received almost $55,000 in royalties over several years from a book he wrote that was published by a friend whose printing company was paid $265,000 by Wright's campaign committee in 1986.

Wright, who had written four other books published by mainstream publishers, received a 55 percent royalty for this book, compared to usual royalties of 15 percent. The book seemed a possible scheme to launder campaign contributions. It wasn't. The money Wright's campaign paid Moore was fully accounted for. Moore himself had suggested that Wright write the book, and Moore made a substantial profit on it. But other reporters began sniffing around. They turned up another problem.

Earlier the *Wall Street Journal*'s Brooks Jackson had written a major investigative piece about Wright and had failed to uncover anything new. But he would later uncover the fact that several lobbyists had bought 1,000 copies of Wright's book. These sales did not violate House ethics rules, which specifically exempted book royalties from any limitations. It was in the past. And lobbyists were allowed to give members of Congress honoraria of $2,000 to make a speech; Wright's defenders argued the book purchases were less of a conflict of interest than honoraria.

Yet, legal or not, this was a way for lobbyists to funnel money to Wright. It was clearly inappropriate. Wright had just provided Gingrich with resonance.

"The book was just lagniappe," Gingrich said later, using a New Orleans expression for something extra which was unexpected. "I was going to proceed regardless, but it certainly helped."

While he sowed seeds among major media outlets, he simultaneously pursued an alternative route. Story ideas travel in two directions, from national to local, and the reverse. If a story appeared often enough in different local media, eventually national reporters would pick it up. Then, when something national did appear, it would rekindle local interest, perhaps an editorial. And local markets were easier to crack; a member of the House, even one from out-of-town, was a bigger deal locally than in Washington. "I'm trying to create a resonance out there," he said. "When something moves on the wire there will be echoes."

Gingrich was relentless and built a network of resonance in every possible public outlet. Chase Manhattan Bank head Willard Butcher made a speech on ethics. Radio commentator Paul Harvey talked about it on the air. Owen Frisby, a lobbyist for Chase, sent Gingrich a transcript of Harvey's remarks. Gingrich wrote to Frisby and Butcher asking, "Let me know what you think of the pattern of on-going corruption in the U.S. House of Representatives."

And wherever Gingrich traveled for a speech—and he traveled often—he would talk about corruption in the House, and the corruption of Jim Wright. He told his audiences to write letters to the editor of their local newspapers, to call in on talk shows, to demand answers from their local Congressional representatives in public meetings, *What are you doing about Jim Wright?* And he told people to write Common Cause.

He also sought out local reporters and editorial writers, and urged them to look into Wright. Perhaps the local paper would write an editorial condemning the way Jim Wright ran the House, or, better yet, about corruption in the House, or about Wright himself. Perhaps local reporters would write about Wright's affairs. Perhaps they would raise the issue with local members of Congress. To get people in a district talking about something—that was the way to get that member's attention.

Gingrich both repeated his now-old line, "Jim Wright is the most corrupt Speaker in the twentieth century"—the comment had an authoritative, academic precision to it that lent it credibility—and escalated it. A story in the *Miami Herald* was a perfect example of how Gingrich used the media.

Gingrich went to Miami to give a speech to a local Republican group, which had offered an interview with him to Tom Fiedler, the paper's political editor. That much was routine. But it was not routine for Gingrich to come to the paper, come to Fiedler. "You almost always go see the person you're interviewing," Fiedler said. Fiedler speculated that Gingrich came to the paper to meet with the editorial board; virtually every newspaper has such a group, which usually ranges from half a dozen to twenty people and which often sits down with major figures in different fields for free-ranging discussions.

But that was not the case. There was no such editorial board meeting with Gingrich. Gingrich went to the paper to make sure the interview took place. Reporters are inundated with press releases and suggestions that they interview someone; they often agree to attend such and such a press conference but do not because something more immediate comes up. Gingrich knew if he went to the newsroom, someone, whether it was Fiedler or not, would interview him.

In the interview, Gingrich attacked Wright personally, on the record, in words that would violate House rules if voiced on the floor of the House.

In his story Fiedler quoted Gingrich: "Wright is so consumed by his own power that he is like Mussolini. . . . We have overwhelming evidence that this is a genuinely bad man . . . money laundering . . . a genuinely corrupt man." Fiedler also wrote that "Wright, according to published accounts, used his influence to block federal investigations into the lending practices of friends and supporters. . . . Gingrich said his charges are based on numerous news accounts." But those "news accounts" of accusations were generated by Gingrich himself.

The *Miami Herald* was arguably the best paper in the South. After Fiedler wrote his story, his editor read it and initially declined to run it.

It included no news, only Gingrich's quotes. The editor asked Fiedler why the paper should allow itself to be used by someone who simply wanted to undermine Wright. Fiedler later recalled, "I said that congressmen did not say such things about other congressmen, much less about the Speaker. The fact that one congressman would attack the Speaker, the brutality of the quote, that was a significant part of the news value."

It was *all* of the "news value." Gingrich's charges were headlined and circulated throughout Florida, and reached Washington through the Knight-Ridder bureau; other editors and reporters read the story. It created resonance.

The number-one fact about the news media is that they love fights, Gingrich had said. *When you give them confrontations you get attention.*

Gingrich's aide Karen Van Brocklin immediately added this *Herald* story to the clip file as further evidence of Wright's corruption. It would be handed to every reporter who contacted Gingrich, who explained, "My technique is simple. If I can get the news media focused, he will become so expensive for the Democratic Party, it will keep him out of the chair [of the 1988 Democratic Convention]."

Gingrich hoped to have some impact on the presidential election. Just raising the issue deflected attention from what pundits had already termed "the sleaze factor," the criminal convictions of senior Reagan aides entirely independent of the Iran-contra scandal. On November 30, 1987, Gingrich wrote Iowa GOP Congressman Tom Tauke to suggest, "An Iowa-focused effort the first week or ten days of January on whether Jim Wright is too corrupt to be chairman of the Democratic National Convention would be *very helpful*" [his italics].

The national press would be swarming over Iowa in early January, getting ready for the presidential caucuses a few weeks later.

Then, in mid-December, Gingrich sent out a "Dear Colleague" letter to every member of the House, proposing an investigation of Wright. He included with his letter a five-page collection of negative quotes from *Newsweek,* the *Wall Street Journal,* the *Washington Post,* and other papers. He also included a story from *Regardie's,* a local Washington magazine that has since ceased publication, accusing Wright of intervening to protect outright crooks in the savings and loan industry. The title of the *Regardie's* story was "The Speaker and the Sleaze/ The story of how two good old boys from the Lone Star State—one who loved power and one who loved money—tried to corrupt the thrift industry." The magazine made it seem that Wright and the savings and loan owner it termed "the sleaze" were close friends. Yet Wright had never even met the man.

Gingrich also held a press conference, released the Dear Colleague letter, and demanded that the House Committee on Standards of Official Conduct, the formal name for the Ethics Committee, investigate Wright.

Gingrich attacked Wright viciously, particularly on his savings and loan involvement and his book. Later it was learned that Gingrich had questionable book arrangements himself. Shortly before winning election to Congress in 1978, his supporters had set up a limited partnership which paid him $13,000 to write a novel. They received tax deductions; he never turned in a manuscript. In 1984, he did publish *Window of Opportunity*, a political tract. He received a standard royalty, but political supporters again set up a limited partnership, this time raising $105,000 to promote the book, while paying his wife over $10,000 to administer the money. At least one conservative group bought the book in bulk. In addition, Gingrich ran a political action committee created to support conservative candidates. It raised $217,868 but distributed only $900 to candidates. The rest went either for fund-raising expenses or for Gingrich's own expenses.

Had reporters known of Gingrich's unusual arrangements at the time, some would have dismissed his attacks on Wright and not written a story at all. Others would have referred snidely to Gingrich's book deals, implying hypocrisy and pure partisanship. But they did not know. And when a member of Congress called for an investigation of the Speaker of the House, that was news.

Gingrich's press conference and Dear Colleague added a chill to the House. One Democratic member said, "*Regardie's* has to make you wonder. There are other things. Stenholm agreed to support the budget in return for help on cutting appropriations. He was screwed. I've been finessed. I'm not sure how. Never have I seen as much difference between what I'm being told we've done this year up here—how great it's been, how much we've accomplished—and what my constituents say back home. If more people than I feel this way, he's in trouble."

Others did feel that way. A chill descended on the House. One Wright ally said, "People tell Wright no one's talking about this. That's true, but only because it's an unwritten rule about not making negative comments about colleagues. These backbenchers, a lot of them are more moral than the guys making all the speeches. They sit there saying nothing, but if a problem comes up they'll pounce."

After Gingrich's public call for an Ethics Committee investigation, Wright sat at breakfast with a cool anger. He had just watched a segment on *Good Morning, America* about the criminal trials of Reagan intimates Mike Deaver and Lyn Nofziger. Three times a Republican had thrown Wright's name into the conversation, and a Democrat had not responded.

Some members had in fact jumped to Wright's defense. Others believed the best strategy was silence, that Gingrich wanted a confrontation to generate more publicity. Others did not know enough of the facts to want to stick their necks out defending Wright.

Wright wanted to present the facts. His staff was preparing a detailed answer to all the charges. But that would take a month. Wright wanted to take the floor immediately to respond.

"Find me parliamentary justification in the *Regardie's* story to claim a point of personal privilege," he told his senior staff at breakfast. Wright's voice was cold and definite. A point of personal privilege would give him one hour of floor time. "You tell me not to respond to Gingrich? I'll respond to the story, not to him. My colleagues have not been given the information with which to defend me. You folks talked me out of writing a letter to *Regardie's*. You'll try to talk me out of this."

"Mr. Speaker," an aide said. "We *will* try to talk you out of it. Not one member is talking about this crap. They don't give it any credence."

"Mr. Speaker, please. If you must do something, do it in a Caucus, not the floor. Please, not with cameras, television, reporters."

All day long staff and colleagues urged him, don't make an issue, the stories would go away. *Just let the damn thing lie.* At least wait until they had all the facts, marshaled definitively, to rebut things once and for all. Finally Wright agreed.

But his instinct was to fight back, although he added, "If colleagues had heaped opprobrium on Gingrich, I'd be satisfied. But they haven't. The only way he'll stop is pressure from his colleagues."

His assumption about collegial pressure was right. Gingrich was alert to it; he did not want to destroy himself. "I've watched colleagues' body language toward me," he said. "It's actually improved. If I had gone after

O'Neill this hard, I would have been a social outcast.... Wright should get a solid 'A' for performance. As a technician of power, he's done a great job. The down-side is, he's a loner still. There's no deep body of affection for him. Being a loner eliminates a safety net both of information and good will."

In December, Foley had spoken to Michel and Cheney—not Lott—about Gingrich's activities; he had not threatened them, had simply asked, "Is this what the House is coming to? This kind of vituperation?"

Foley's comments had registered with Michel, but not with Cheney. Foley believed, "Cheney was deeply angry over the contras." Coelho agreed: "Cheney's changed. I don't know anyone on the Democratic leadership side who feels they can trust him anymore, or that they have his confidence. Cheney was the hit-man for the White House on the contras. The Speaker totally out-maneuvered him. Since then he's been out for vengeance."

To the GOP leadership, Gingrich had become useful. Recognizing how useful, he noted somewhat disdainfully, "They were quite willing for *me* to do this. No one asked me to stop."

By now Gingrich's office had become a clearinghouse. Those with anything negative to say about Wright found their way to it, from his home-town Fort Worth, from the bureaucracy, from personal or political enemies. Van Brocklin then called investigative reporters and gave them the leads to check out. So did Gingrich himself: "I talk routinely with investigative reporters. They call me and I call them."

Then Gingrich accelerated his attacks, contacting major media figures such as David Gergen, editor of *U.S. News and World Report*, who had been communications director in the Reagan White House, arranging to sit down with the *New York Times* editorial board, and appealing to the competitiveness of *Times* editor Abe Rosenthal by writing him, "I'm just puzzled why the *New York Times* hasn't taken on the issue of corruption in the House like the *Washington Post* and the *Wall Street Journal* have."

He talked to Attorney General Ed Meese, who had his own ethics problems and would be eager to divert media attention from himself, left-wing activist Ralph Nader, and organizers of conservative causes. To each he made a different appeal: to Meese, to launch an investigation; to Nader, to help clean up corruption; to conservatives, to help circulate petitions calling for an investigation of Wright.

And he repeatedly pressured Common Cause's head Fred Wertheimer. Common Cause was key: Gingrich needed its nonpartisan credibility. In February Gingrich reminded Wertheimer that in Wertheimer's own letter to the Ethics Committee the past July—this was the letter that followed by eight days, and used much of the language from, Gingrich's letter to Wertheimer—"you stated that, 'The Ethics Committee has abdicated its responsibility. . . .' Your silence in this [Wright] matter weakens the cause of honest government."

A few days later, Gingrich called another press conference and announced that he would file a formal ethics complaint against Wright in March. The *Washington Times* then ran editorials on successive days attacking Wright, helping to build support for filing charges; one was titled "Taken to the Laundry," accusing Wright of laundering campaign contributions.

Then House GOP leader Bob Michel intervened. He sat down with Gingrich in his office and, while not telling him to stop, made clear that this was serious business. He asked Gingrich to allow some people to examine his allegations. Gingrich agreed. Two Republican congressmen, Robert Livingston and James Sensenbrenner, both former prosecutors, and three GOP lawyers familiar with House rules reviewed Gingrich's seven-inch thick file on Wright.

But the file contained only newspaper clippings, and they all covered the same handful of charges. Some stories, such as *Newsweek*'s, specifically stipulated that no evidence of anything illegal had been uncovered. And most charges, even if true, did not violate House rules.

Livingston, Sensenbrenner, and the three lawyers reached the same conclusion: Gingrich had nothing. Michel had them meet in his office with Gingrich. They told him you didn't investigate people just because they did something that didn't look good on the front page of the *Washington Post*. You needed a solid reason. Gingrich's file fell well short.

"What about a grand jury?" Gingrich asked. Going to the Ethics Committee was analogous to going to a grand jury. "Isn't there enough to go to a grand jury?"

Unanimously the lawyers agreed there was not. Later Livingston said, "This was serious. Sometimes you try to do the right thing."

Gingrich returned to his office angry and disturbed. "It was disheartening," his aide Van Brocklin said. "Newt was pretty upset."

But he did not stop. Instead he immediately called a late-night meeting of those working with him. Three things came out of this meeting.

First was an intense effort that lasted several months to dig up new, damaging material on Wright. Daniel Swillinger looked into allegations about Wright's possible involvement in an old scandal, but later had to report, "This whole episode appears to be a dead end." Van Brocklin looked into federally funded projects in Fort Worth, going so far as to investigate the fact that Wright's friends had several parking spaces in a garage partly built with federal funds. Gingrich demanded an explanation from the federal agency overseeing the project, and received a copy of a lease for the spaces. Gingrich himself investigated whether Wright had ever been promoted to a general in the Air Force reserves—that and its pension could make a good story. (He had not been.)

Second was a decision that Swillinger and other attorneys would draft a formal ethics complaint, despite the dismissal of the idea by Livingston and Sensenbrenner.

Third was an even more aggressive media strategy. In the two weeks following this session, Gingrich initiated a blizzard of direct and indirect press contacts. He wrote to Assistant Attorney General William Weld, "May I suggest, the next time the news media asks about corruption in the White House, you ask them about corruption in the Speaker's office," and sent a similar letter to George Bush, then running for President.

He contacted conservative columnist George Will and appealed for his help: "It is frightening to take on this much power, and the ability of the Speaker to protect himself is awesome."

He wrote conservative columnist James Kilpatrick and said bluntly, "Our goal is to establish a news media focus . . . so that members will realize that a public accounting of Wright's personal and financial dealings is necessary."

He contacted *Washington Post* and *New York Times* reporters, editorial writers, and columnists he believed were receptive to his charges. He also asked several conservative political action committees to help him gather petitions calling for an investigation of Wright, and to keep the issue on the front burner among grassroots conservatives.

And he sent out another "Dear Colleague" letter, with of course copies to the press, about the indictment of a major Democratic fund-raiser who was close to Wright. The indictment had nothing to do with any political activities and the man was later acquitted. But Gingrich wrote that the "attached articles . . . are further proof that allegations of unethical and questionable conduct against Speaker Jim Wright need to be investigated."

Lastly, he continued pounding on Wertheimer and Common Cause. On March 11, Gingrich wrote him again. Again, Wertheimer did not respond. Gingrich called. The call was not returned. Gingrich called again, and again, placing a call every day for several weeks. None was ever returned. His staff called Wertheimer's staff; their calls were not returned. That did not matter. Wertheimer was learning about his relentlessness, learning that he would not go away.

Gingrich later explained, "The basic thing we did was emphasize the media. We worked on the assumption that if enough newspapers said there should be an investigation, Common Cause would have to say it. Then members would say it. It would happen."

Wright's staff and attorneys finally finished their defense: a "white paper" providing facts to rebut all of Gingrich charges, backed up by sworn depositions. It was comprehensive and well done.

Cong. Beryl Anthony of Arkansas, head of the Democratic Congressional Campaign Committee, also filed a formal complaint about a PAC Gingrich ran—the one that raised over $200,000 but gave only $900 to candidates—with the Federal Election Commission and asked the Postal Service to investigate possible mail fraud. Meanwhile Gingrich's Georgia GOP colleague Patrick Swindall was indicted for laundering drug money. Wright's people thought those two things would put Gingrich on the defensive. But filing the complaint had neither intimidated Gingrich—he simply denounced it as a smear—nor discredited him. The overwhelming majority of reporters Gingrich continued to contact were unaware of it.

Wright conducted a series of meetings with people he respected inside and outside the House, people like Bob Strauss and John White, both

Texans and former Democratic National Committee chairmen, Wright's senior aides, and several members including Foley and Coelho, who both had excellent relations with and a history of managing the media.

At each meeting Wright said he wanted to defend himself publicly, preferably on the floor of the House.

Each time the group unanimously advised against it. It would just escalate the entire issue, create a round of front page stories. And what if Wright went public and made a mistake in something he said? Any mistake, no matter how minor, could destroy his credibility. The advisers believed that Wertheimer could not get involved even if he wanted to because he would appear partisan. They also knew Livingston and Sensenbrenner had dismissed Gingrich's charges as lacking substance, and believed that that would isolate Gingrich among his colleagues. And if he didn't respond? The consensus was that the issue would go away.

So Wright contained his own instincts and did nothing.

Then the *Washington Post* ran a lengthy story investigating Wright's ties to the savings and loan industry. It was by far the most detailed account of Wright's actions to appear, written by Charles Babcock, the same investigative reporter who had broken the story on his book. But this time Babcock exonerated Wright of any misconduct. The definitive nature of the story and the credibility of the writer added weight to that exoneration. It looked like, finally, the negative stories impugning Wright's ethics were behind them.

The next day Wright's staff was exuberant.

But Gingrich had been in constant touch not only with *Wall Street Journal* investigative reporters, but with the paper's editorial writers. Unlike editorial writers at most newspapers, *Journal* editorial writers did not simply sit back and analyze events of the moment. *Journal* editorial writers mounted editorial campaigns. They created issues and kept them alive. They pounded and pounded and pounded on the same theme. They did not let go. Former *Journal* editorial writer Jude Wanniski had made supply-side economics acceptable and had actively searched in Washington for a champion for his tax-cut ideas, finally finding one in Jack Kemp in the mid-1970s. Kemp had then convinced Ronald Reagan to adopt the idea. Gingrich talked particularly to *Journal* editorial writer John Fund.

So did Van Brocklin, who said, "During some periods I would talk to him every day."

Brooks Jackson, the *Journal* investigative reporter, recalled, "I would talk to Newt and I might say something, or he would say something, and two or three days later I would see the same idea, even the precise same phrase, on our editorial page."

Fund later explained that his disagreements with Wright were "a policy difference primarily." He and Gingrich talked after the *Post* piece. Two days later Fund wrote a *Journal* editorial, conceding, "The timing was somewhat a reaction to the *Post*."

The editorial was titled, "Where's the Investigation?" It ran several thousand words, using up by itself the entire space allotted for editorials that day, reciting almost every allegation Gingrich had ever made against Wright.

The equation of power had changed.

Wright once again met with the same swirling group of advisers down the hall from his office in H-201. Once again he wanted to go to the floor. Once again, unanimously, his advisers argued for silence. Wright was angry. He had been getting that advice for months. Look where it had gotten him. But he took it one more time.

Twice in July, then again in January, February, and March, Gingrich had written Fred Wertheimer demanding that Common Cause call for an investigation. No new facts had come out since then. Except for one curt reply Wertheimer had not responded. A year earlier, however, he had not replied to Gingrich's July 21, 1987, letter, but eight days later he had borrowed much of Gingrich's language and most of his charges about several members of congress, putting them into his own letter to the Ethics Committee.

Still, Wertheimer and others at Common Cause were troubled by questions that Wright had not answered. There was also Gingrich's relentless pounding. "I think," Gingrich said, "Wertheimer may have intuited that the next phase was a *Wall Street Journal* editorial saying, 'Why Is Common Cause Afraid of Jim Wright?'"

A man who sometimes cooperated with Wertheimer said, "I think Fred started worrying about his money people."

Eight days after the *Journal* editorial demanding an investigation, Wertheimer wrote a letter to Ethics Committee chairman Julian Dixon. A copy of the letter arrived in Wright's office by messenger at 10:00 A.M., shortly before its release to the media. It addressed two issues: whether Wright's book was a scheme for converting campaign funds to personal use; and whether "he sought to obtain special treatment in connection of the regulatory activities of the Federal Home Loan Bank Board for... party campaign contributors."

Wertheimer later told reporters that Common Cause acted because Wright had not answered the charges in the press.

The letter demanded an investigation, conducted by an outside counsel, of Speaker of the House Jim Wright.

Wertheimer's call was a front-page story in the *Washington Post,* the *New York Times,* the *Los Angeles Times,* the *Boston Globe,* and every major paper in the country. NBC, CBS, ABC, CNN, the MacNeil-Lehrer show, Ted Koppel's *Nightline,* all featured the story prominently. Perhaps the most extreme story appeared the *New Republic,* which even accused Wright of having supported the Vietnam War—which his son had fought in—because the army bought thousands of helicopters made in Fort Worth.

Gingrich did not stop. Judy Hughes, chair of the National Federation of Republican Women, assured him "The Federation's 160,000 members are ready to aid you in your battle against Speaker Wright." The Conservative Campaign Fund and Citizens for Reagan sent a mailing to all Republican House candidates saying: "We write to encourage you to make... House Speaker Jim Wright a major issue in your campaign. Should Wright appear in your district, you face an opportunity to turn an honor for your opponent into an embarrassment."

Gingrich also tried to keep Wright an issue in presidential politics, asking if Democratic presidential nominee Michael Dukakis "agree[s] with Common Cause that there is sufficient reason for a formal investigation of the Speaker? Will he allow Speaker Wright to chair the Democratic National Convention if he is under investigation?"

A reporter asked George Bush about Attorney General Ed Meese's continued ethics problems. Bush, who then trailed Dukakis by sixteen points in the polls, snapped, "You talk about Ed Meese. How about talking about what Common Cause raised about the Speaker the other day?

Are they going to go for an independent counsel so the nation will have this full investigation? Why don't people call out for that? I will right now. I think they ought to."

Bush cited other House members who should be investigated. All were Democrats, all were on Gingrich's list.

That night, May 24, Republicans attacked Wright from a different tack. Cheney had organized a "special order" over C-SPAN to condemn the way Democrats ran the House. One after another, Republicans got up to complain about the Democrats' and Wright's exercise of power. Several days later *Washington Post* columnist David Broder, perhaps the single most influential political reporter in Washington, wrote a column entitled "How About a Little Glasnost for the House?" and repeated many of the points made in the special order.

Early in the morning on May 26, 1988, in the hallway outside the Sergeant of Arms office a few cameras and reporters waited for Gingrich to arrive. Across the corridor and behind closed doors was where Wright breakfasted every morning. The mood at breakfast was somber, the only sounds the clicking of silverware. Wright aide Marshall Lynam walked in and hissed, "The vultures have gathered outside, I see."

Gingrich walked into the office with his papers. The room resembled an old-fashioned bank, with a marble-topped counter and a row of barred openings, behind which tellers cashed checks for House employees. Gingrich pushed open a gate, sat down at a desk, had his papers notarized, then, with a Capitol policeman trailing him, walked down to the terrace level to the Ethics Committee office. There the corridor was packed. He walked inside, closed the door—the press remained outside—and handed his charges to a receptionist, who stamped them with the date and time of receipt. Then he walked outside and held a press conference.

Earlier, Ted Koppell had said to Gingrich that he seemed isolated, that no Republican had joined him. The next morning during a quorum call Cheney had walked up to Gingrich and said, "You're not alone."

Seventy-one Republicans signed a letter urging "further inquiry into the activities of Speaker Jim Wright."

Wright had made his bed, now let him lie in it.

The next day, Ronald Reagan declared, "I think it is proper that there is an investigation going forward. . . . I think that everyone would feel that it was more proper if it was done by an investigator outside—an appointed investigator."

George Bush was also telling reporters, "I want to see Michael Dukakis join me—he seems to be talking about ethics all the time, and why doesn't he just get in there and join me in suggesting we have an independent counsel for the House?"

The President of the United States, seconded by the Vice President of the United States, his party's presidential nominee, had gotten involved. The story stayed alive. The pressure on the committee intensified.

Now the *New York Times* lead editorial, entitled "Speaker Wright's Ghostly Ethics," called for an investigation. Wright saw it and his expression froze. *What did they know about him? What did they know about any of it?*

Gingrich meanwhile sent out a fund-raising letter for a PAC requesting help in his "difficult and politically costly fight." He asked not only for money, but for people to deluge the Ethics Committee with demands for an investigation of Jim Wright.

Once again Wright told his staff, "I want to get my side out. I am ready to start a counterattack. I'm tired of waiting. We've prepared this damn document, now I want it told."

His staff still objected, one of them warning, "You may raise questions the Ethics Committee has not thought of. Wait for them."

"I've been listening to that counsel for a year. Where has it put me? My enemies have been maligning me. I want to get my side out, in detail. I hire all these former journalists, think they know the press, ask them what to do, and get this advice and it does not work. I wanted to take the floor last year on a point of personal privilege. 'No, no, don't do that,' everyone told me. 'This story will die.' Well it didn't die. There is only one way through this. Straight through it. I don't want to hang back anymore."

Later that day his advisers continued urging him to remain silent until everything had surfaced. "I don't recall a single piece of advice, not one, to go public," said one man who attended virtually every meeting.

Meanwhile the Ethics Committee reviewed Gingrich's complaint. It was the same as it had been when Livingston and Sensenbrenner had examined it. The committee could have dismissed it, as Livingston and Sensenbrenner and the three other GOP lawyers had. Wright asked the committee to hear his rebuttal before they decided whether to proceed. The Ethics Committee would not hear him and would not dismiss the complaint.

The investigation would proceed.

Livingston said in a tone of disgust, "The investigation happened because Gingrich was able to manipulate the press."

THE
OLYMPIANS

These chapters too involve power, both the physical power of the athlete and political power. We begin with the athlete.

Perhaps it is the pagan in all of us, the wish to exult joyously in the physical, that makes us respect—and in moments of fantasy envy—athletes. Especially champions. The way they let everything go and hurl all of themselves, minds and bodies, at a target is proof of a freedom, a simplicity, a purity that the rest of us seek. We envy their wildness, their risking, and we envy that they are the best, the very best, at what they do. Few of us are willing to pursue such a goal; instead we settle for the comfortable and secure and safe, avoiding defeat. But we also avoid victory. So we vicariously run with them, leap with them, win with them, and we are a little in awe of and frightened by their intensity.

The athletes care little about our vicarious thrills. They do not pursue excellence for us. They seek it for themselves.

Even world class athletes do not all enjoy the adulation of crowds. I recall planning to write about a woman who set a world record in the woman's walk, then deciding the event didn't justify doing so. When I told her, she said, "I understand." Yet she was as dedicated as anyone.

What all of these athletes share is a desire to be the best in the world. They also share a respect for other athletes, for others who are willing to make the sacrifices and stand revealed.

All of these athletes had one goal: to win a medal in the Olympics—the 1980 Olympics hosted by the Soviet Union. Their stories demonstrate quite directly how politics intervenes in our daily lives, even when it seems remote.

RENALDO NEHEMIAH

R enaldo Nehemiah is simply the best there is and the best there ever was. In the world of track and field he is king. Emperor. At the pinnacle of all amateur sport. No one else has ever set such a run of world records—five times in five months he has set new world records.

"I'm doing things no one has ever done," he says. "No one else has come close. I'm the first person to do unheard-of feats more or less consecutively."

He is nineteen years old.

His sport is not gymnastics, where bodyweight-to-strength ratios make the triumph of teenage girls not only possible but likely, or even swimming, where twenty-three-year-old athletes are long past their prime. He is a hurdler, a sport in which athletes usually peak in their late twenties. Confronting hurdle after hurdle, each one 3'6" high, at full speed requires fearlessness, which is a function of character and not age. (To the extent it does depend on age, youth's sense of invulnerability gives him an advantage in this area, too.) But success requires also speed, power, technique, and the maturity to wage psychological warfare against rivals. Those are all things that usually reach their peak only with years of work and experience.

What makes him phenomenal, however, is not his talent and work ethic, but his ego—ego in the large sense.

It is not that he is one of those spoiled athletes who respect no one else, who believe they can get away with anything, who behave as if the rest of the world exists to fulfill their needs. Far from it. Yet his ego informs and controls everything he does.

In these past months when he set world record after world record "everything was at my control. I planned everything that I did—weightlifting, training, everything. . . . I consider myself a technician. I try to stay in control of myself at all times, knowing my every move, my every reaction."

Nehemiah, says his coach Frank Costello, himself once a world-class high jumper, "knows what he wants and what sacrifices he must make to get it."

To handle the world he has devised a system, disciplining himself and using the formality of that discipline to keep the world at bay. Everything he does fits into the system. He hurdles precisely and dresses neatly. He is unrelentingly courteous, and courtesy defines patterns; when someone holds a door for him, a "thank-you" always follows. Never does he talk of "school" or "college" or even "Maryland"; always he uses the complete formal phrase, "the University of Maryland." He considers himself "a student at the University of Maryland," and "the University of Maryland track team is" going to this meet or that meet.

His control over himself and everything around him, his faith in his own judgement even on technical issues, make it difficult to remember— he is nineteen years old.

A sophomore at the University of Maryland, handsome, a little over six feet tall, an African American of medium complexion, Nehemiah is neither broad-shouldered nor thickly muscled. But when he moves, when he opens a door or takes a step, his physical grace makes him look the athlete. He is of course a great athlete.

There are two types of great athletes. The first seems to melt into the sport and become one with it: long-jumpers who love to get up, into the wind and air, and to whom each contact with the earth is a regretful reminder of mortality; basketball players who have the soft hands, the soft touch, who pass to the open man, never force a shot, take the lay-up rather than the dunk, make the foul shots look easy, and who fit so completely into the flow of the game that their contribution seems almost invisible. Only the statistics—say for example thirty-eight points, eleven assists—reveal their achievements.

Nehemiah is not one of these.

Then there is the second type who conquers the sport, who dominates and smothers and defeats it.

Such is Nehemiah. He is an ego demanding a place. A very private person, described as a "loner," he is an intruder in the world outside and wants not to join with it or fit into the flow of the world but to conquer it. His sensitivity, his awareness, is to and of his own body. All else is external.

The hurdle is the enemy. It is high enough to force a runner to break stride, high enough in fact to present a real obstacle, even a threatening obstacle, and the hurdles present themselves one after another after another.

"I think of the hurdle," he says, "as a barrier that's in the way. My main objective is to get over it without hurting myself. A lot of hurdlers fear that barrier...I don't feel inferior to the hurdle. The hurdle has a lot of control over the race—it's 90 percent of it—but I don't feel inferior to it."

It is something else to conquer, another part of the outside. His ego is at war with the external. He wants no one except himself to benefit from his performances. Track is an individual sport, and he does not even pay lip service to the usual cliches about teammates or coaches.

"I'm selfish," he concedes. "When I run I'm representing myself—different people get credit for it. The University of Maryland. But I represent myself."

His ego also creates central tensions in his life—between insiders and outsiders, between a desire for the world's attention and a desire to be left alone.

In fact, he has received extraordinary attention. His coach Frank Costello points to a stack of envelopes on his desk. "These are all requests for interviews that won't be granted, including *Newsweek*. They've been cutting into his workouts, cutting into school. There are tons more requests than you can comprehend."

"The pressure's so much," Nehemiah is saying, shaking his head. Not to perform in the hurdles, but to reveal himself, to fulfill the role of a celebrity. "People wanting to know everything. Indoors I got really upset. I came to practice two days before a big meet and there were five or six TV stations. . . . It got to the point where I almost dreaded coming to practice."

Yet he simultaneously demands recognition.

He complains that his world records haven't made the cover of *Sports Illustrated*, and wonders what he has "to do to get more outright attention. I was the best hurdler in history, and it's so low-keyed. I ran so well week after week it just sort of died. Like if I didn't break the world record, people thought I had a bad meet."

When he spends a full hour ignoring a writer who had an appointment with him while he stretches and warms up, the writer finally says, "You know we don't have to do this."

Nehemiah shakes his head, tells the writer not to leave, that he knows the publicity helps him. But he doesn't apologize. From his perspective the writer is just one more person gaining some benefit from him. He is right, but he recognizes the symbiotic nature of the relationship. To say he is wise beyond his years understates his calm.

His answers to questions are considered carefully before he speaks—even for the automatic answers, and many answers are automatic, like those of a politician who repeats the same thing over and over to each new reporter and makes it sound fresh. But he isn't a politician. He has been asked so many questions so many times, been probed so constantly, one has to have sympathy for him. Everyone wants a piece of him. He is reluctant to give it.

The courtesy, the carefully defined patterns of speech and behavior, protect his privacy and soften his aloofness. It allows him to reconcile his desire for attention—even adulation—and still keep the world at bay. He is in a splendid and glorious isolation; his contact with the world comes at precise points, rigidly defined, as in geometry where a line becomes tangent to a circle.

Yet there are gray areas. There are insiders—other athletes, a few friends—who seem to have penetrated the courtesies. Without question Nehemiah is well liked by his teammates. There are casual, easy-going friendly exchanges and acceptance of each other.

"You go to that party?" he is asked.

"No, but I heard about it."

"You coming over then?"

"I think so."

With them he has an easy grace and a quick smile. It is not that success has gone to his head. Rather, one reason for his success is that same sense of self, that same control. Besides, there is a girl. The isolation is not absolute.

It is only the rest of the world that is outside. It is only the rest of the world he wants to beat.

Nehemiah is jogging languidly around the track in tandem with another runner on as close to an off day as he has. Their strides mirror each other's, their feet land side by side simultaneously, like a drill team in perfect step, and moving so slowly that a jogger in street clothes and sneakers easily keeps pace. Even when they accelerate and run hard for three hundred yards, leaving the jogger far behind, their strides remain matched. They glide.

Nehemiah is running with grace and power, yet so is the other athlete. It would be untrue to say Nehemiah stands out, is clearly superior, when he only jogs or strides or even runs hard. Oh, he is good. Yet others look as good. Other great athletes run on this track, including at least three other potential Olympians. But then, while he strides with his training partner around the track, he casually, almost as an afterthought, whips his rear leg up high and tight to his buttocks as though clearing a hurdle.

The suddenness of it! The quick power of the move and the quick return to a smooth rhythm! As easily and quickly as he picked his leg up, just that quickly he has separated himself from everyone else on the track. Suddenly he is not like everyone else.

He doesn't want to be like everyone else. He wants everyone else to make way. He likes the spotlight. He likes the pressure. Last year he was ranked number one in the world. Even so, this year, before his string of world records began, he says, "I had to prove myself all over again. I have to prove myself every meet. I have to prove it to the media, to people—I know I'm the best, but I have to prove it to them. After 1980 there'll be nothing left to prove. Then they'll know."

LINDA DRAGAN

Ft. McNair in Washington is not the usual army post. Only a few blocks from the U.S. Capitol and the White House, its manicured lawns decorate the homes of three- and four-star generals who make decisions about national policy. But like other posts it has a gym.

Today it is raining, a heavy steady drenching rain, cold and desolate feeling, the kind of rain that makes people dream of hot chocolate. Linda Dragan has just jogged through the rain from her car to the gym where she is arguing with the attendant to let her stay. She represented the United States of America as a member of the last two Olympic teams and has trained at Ft. McNair for months for next year's Olympics. But she has no military identification, and her training partner, who does, is late. The attendant doesn't care about the fact that he has seen Dragan before or her Olympic past, and orders her to wait outside in the rain. Dragan refuses angrily.

The attendant threatens to call the MPs. "Go ahead," Dragan says. She is twenty-six years old, a broad-shouldered woman, bulky and not traditionally feminine and yet with an odd suggestion of grace, and she is just stubborn enough to dig in. The attendant calls the MPs.

Three arrive. They take Dragan outside—not into the rain but into their patrol car—and start to interrogate her. Just then her partner arrives, flashes his ID, and the MPs let her go.

"Look," Dragan snorts, "I was happy they didn't handcuff me."

Reaching the Olympics requires a long and tortuous route for any athlete; for those in the less-publicized sports the route is longer, and more tortuous.

Renaldo Nehemiah complains that *Sports Illustrated* has not yet put him on the cover. The only contact Linda Dragan will ever have with the magazine is if she buys it.

Dragan races kayaks—she paddles sleek narrow splinters of mahogany through the water. It is not a new sport; every Olympiad has included it. It is simply one of those sports so unknown that it escapes even the catholicity of the weekend network sport shows.

But getting into a gym to train with weightlifting equipment is hardly Dragan's biggest problem. Nor is time, although she is a graduate student at the University of Maryland trying to write a master's thesis, train two to three hours a day, and work as a waitress. Her biggest problem is money.

Early in March she went to Florida for a training camp with the rest of the national team. She was given five dollars a day for expenses. Last year she was one of a four-member U.S. boat team that won the Pan American championship in Mexico City and broke the course record held by the Olympic champions.

"That trip cost me five hundred dollars," Dragan says. "I was told it would be refunded. I haven't seen a penny of the refund yet. I borrowed the money from my granny. I only have one granny. How much can I borrow from her?

"Last December I didn't have money hardly to eat on. I lost my car. I didn't have anything. When I went to the training camp in March, I lost my job. I don't tell employers anymore that I'm an athlete. If they know, they won't hire you. I wondered back then, especially in December: What am I doing this for? I know there's no future in it. If I had any brains I wouldn't be doing it. But I haven't reached my goal yet. My goal is to win an Olympic medal."

She got into kayaking late. As a child she was a swimmer who won her first medal at age five, and in national competition at age ten she placed third in the breast stroke and fifth in the backstroke. "When I was in grade school, I could do more pull-ups than the boys. I always thought it was neat to be strong."

Two of her brothers went to college on football scholarships, and all through school she swam, or played basketball, or ice-skated. But she did not paddle. In college, no longer willing to face what to her had become drudgery, she stopped competing in swimming. She did not paddle either. She partied.

"I got thrown out of school. Nothing much, just for a semester." But that left her hanging around Washington in September 1971. "One day my father put me in the car and told me I was going to the Olympics."

A kayaker, Nancy Leahy, needed a partner. Dragan's father took Linda to the Washington Canoe Club after he had talked to Nancy's father.

"Nancy said the idea of me going to the Olympics was ridiculous. The trials were only ten months away, and I had never even been in a kayak. But she said if I wanted to go out on the water, she'd go out with me."

Both of them made that Olympic team, in a two-person boat.

Dragan turned out to be a natural. She also made the following Olympic team with another partner. For the next one she plans to compete by herself, in singles, believing she now has enough experience and technique that she is coming into her own.

She talks casually of her accomplishments and plans. No hint of the effort, of the pain, of the sacrifice necessary to compete at the international level leaks out. For this is not a sport with either direct or indirect pay-offs. There are no adoring crowds, no endorsement deals, no over or under the table pay-offs.

She calls herself "lazy," says she doesn't train "very hard, certainly not as hard as I should." She jokes about her size—5'6" and 160 pounds: "After every workout we go to Georgetown for ice cream." She makes it all seem so simple, so matter-of-fact. "I always thought if I talked about it I was showing off."

She makes it sound simple, but beneath her accomplishments lies a hardness. Two hardnesses actually. One, an awareness of how pointless and ephemeral her athletic experience may seem to that part of the world called "real." The future is a recurrent theme in her conversation, and she believes hers lies in teaching and coaching.

Dragan wants to be like everyone else. Yet she talks of pushing on to the 1984 Olympics, knowing that each day of training delays her finishing her thesis, and each interruption of the normal career progression separates her from everyone else. When will she start teaching? When can she? And through her talk of being like everyone else and of the future runs an undercurrent of fear that she may be left behind.

The fear has not yet reached the level of desperation, yet it is as if she knows she should give the sport up, but will not. "Practically everyone else my age still paddling is either rich or has a sponsor," she says. Then she shrugs. If she has neither money nor sponsor, what of it? The world owes her nothing. She can take care of herself.

Which is her second hardness, her toughness. When she misses a lift in her weight workout, she is silent, intensely silent for a moment. In that moment she goes inside herself. The mask of her face goes blank and she withdraws from those around her. She says nothing at all for a few minutes, while conversation of others continues. But even the guard who earlier had tried to expel her watches her. She is disciplined. She will not attempt the weight again—it is not part of her planned workout. She doesn't like it, her hatred of the failure makes her want to try it again and succeed. But she is too disciplined for that, too disciplined to break the pattern of this workout. She only gets one chance in competition as well. But the failure visibly burns. Finally she relaxes. Her smile returns. But not until after her next exercise, when she turns her intensity onto it and easily does what she had expected to be hard.

She is isolated. Perhaps all the athletes in her sport are like this. The sport itself is so isolated from the mainstream of athletics in this country. But Dragan has isolated herself beyond that. She and her current partner train by themselves even though other kayakers train with a coach at her own club.

"Well," Dragan says, "He's a great guy and doing a lot for the sport, but let's just say we use different methods. Mine work for me. Maybe his work for him."

From the army to the navy. The David Taylor Model Basin is a top secret navy facility where model warship designs are tested in a tank half a mile long. Through some personal connections to high-ranking officers the Washington Canoe Club has access to it, and with the Potomac River frozen over Dragan is training in it now. It is dark inside, dimly lighted, and the water is black and still. Her kayak is a thin sliver of molded polyester resin and cloth weighing only twenty-six pounds. In international competition she races in a wood boat, but wood boats require a lot of maintenance so she trains in a fiberglass one. It is no sportsman's canoe. It is as slender as a splinter. Simply to sit in a competitive racing kayak without rolling it over marks an achievement of balance. But as soon as Dragan takes her seat, both she and the kayak seem transformed. Her wide powerful hips and shoulders seem smoother, and the kayak seems suddenly alive, light and alert and alive. When Dragan starts to paddle and the kayak moves, she and it merge into something... *sleek.*

In the dark, in the silence, the only sound is that of her paddle breaking water. There is not even the sound of a splash, only a lap-lap-lap as the kayak skims across the surface. Dragan seems at home. Dragan is at home.

She is sitting in the kayak looking up. The kayak continues to glide through the dark water. "The Hungarian coach believes in me. He thinks if anyone can beat the East Germans, I can."

She smiles modestly, then returns her concentration to the paddle, and regains her rhythm and grace. There is no worry about, no thought of, the financial problems or the future. All that slips into her wake.

"When I race," she says, "I start out counting strokes, concentrating on technique. Twenty-three strokes is one hundred meters. The course is five hundred meters. But about halfway through I always lose count. I become aware only of my arms—how they hurt!—and my breathing. Then I'm not aware of anything. Not even of the water. All there is in the world narrows down to faster! faster! *faster!*"

MICHAEL STORM

H ere is this young man from Arlington, Virginia, a suburb of
Washington. Blond, wearing a Harris tweed jacket and penny
loafers, sitting in his fraternity lounge at the University of
Pennsylvania where the big question is: Will the cook quit? Mike Storm
is mildly concerned, says she's a good cook, yet he is uninvolved. He is
uninvolved in much of the normal give and take of socializing. There is
coolness and detachment about him. His fraternity brothers call him
"Stranger."

With a highly compartmentalized life, he has little time for the trivial. He is pursuing two discrete academic programs, one in premed, the
other at the Wharton School of Finance.

"I like the stimulation of the academic environment," he says. "I'm
interested in how the world works."

Of average height, about 5'11", and weighing only about 150 pounds,
he seems more likely to be on his way to Wall Street or the Senate than
the Olympics. Which may be why his sport is the "modern pentathlon."

The modern pentathlon is different from other Olympic events. It consists of riding, fencing, shooting, a 300-meter swim and a 4,000-meter
cross-country run. Added to the Olympics in 1912 to "bring the armies
of the world closer together," the sport still reeks of the fox hunt, of an
officer class. The United States has only two training centers for the
sport: one run by the army in San Antonio and another funded by John
duPont at his farm on Philadelphia's Main Line. (This is the same duPont
who a decade later was arrested for murdering an Olympic wrestler who
trained at the complex.) And where a basic element of all other sports is
youth or play—at least an exultation in the physical—the pentathlon is
based on war. It is indeed how the world works.

"Getting to meet your competitors is always a delicate thing," Storm says. "The sport is eloquent and classical. It's of such an eclectic nature. It's exciting, not in the sense of a roller coaster ride, but in that it's so totally fulfilling."

There are few competitors in this country. It would seem that one need not, therefore, be that great an athlete to get to the Olympics. "But it's not like golf," Storm snorts. "You don't do it unless you're extremely serious and intent.... The sport, the whole concept of the sport, takes such an all-around athlete. It's not a jack-of-all-trades kind of thing. I can't emphasize that enough. To be good in the pentathlon you have to be almost at the national level in five events."

Make no mistake. Mike Storm is an athlete. In age-group swimming competition he was ranked in the top ten nationally in three events; he won the junior national fencing championship (in epee) in 1978, and will have the opportunity to compete at the junior nationals three more times; at the National Sports Federation Games held last summer, he was the only athlete among hundreds to compete in two sports.

In pentathlon international competition he won the juniors and placed fourth in the seniors last year in Austria, while the next highest American finished tenth and the defending national champion placed fourteenth. In January at an international meet in Australia, he won both the junior and senior competitions. And he has achieved all this in quick time. Prior to being invited to a training camp four years ago, he had never fenced, ridden, or shot. Storm is a natural. His mind, in particular, is matched to this event.

All athletic competition has a mental element and it is often the decisive element, but perhaps nothing else requires quite the mental discipline, quite the versatility, and quite the sustained concentration of the pentathlon. Each event markedly differs from the others. Major meets run five days, one day for each event. To persist over that long a period demands extreme discipline and both mental and physical acuity and flexibility: an athlete might ride for only twenty minutes the first day, but the next day fence for hours.

There is only one chance to ride, only one chance to shoot. It is as if a batter got only one pitch to hit in a game, as if a pole vaulter got only one jump, instead of three at each height. The intensity of it keeps coming. Day after day after day after day after day, waiting to compete, waiting to compete and then—abruptly—it's all over. There is a void, an emptiness, after each event. Yet that void must be overcome to meet the next day's competition.

"One mistake," Storm says, "and a year's training goes for nought."

When Storm was fifteen years old and first exposed to the pentathlon at the training camp, the sport drew him to it, whispered in his ear, seduced him. It demands so much. It demands his mind, and it demands his body. He realized he could be good and even then began to point to the Olympics. He observes, "I don't think one continues in such a sport unless one has a singular goal."

Now Storm is nineteen. The current world champion is thirty-eight. It would seem that Storm has time to achieve that goal. Yet for all his coolness and detachment, for all the surgical dispassion of his speech, he is passionate. He is intense. And he is best in the two events which demand the most concentration, fencing and shooting.

His fencing coach at Penn, Dave Micahnik, who himself competed in three Olympics, believes Storm could compete internationally in fencing alone. In the pentathlon, one touch determines the winner, and there is a three-minute time limit. If the time expires without either competitor touching the other, both lose. Yet the fencing lasts twelve to fourteen hours because there may be as many as sixty competitors and each athlete is matched against every other.

Storm likes the time limit. "It increases the intensity. As seconds tick away the opponent gets nervous, comes at you wildly. I'll run the time out to get that. The fencing is so—you have to put everything into one touch. It becomes very heated."

And then the kill. Fencing is a physical chess game.

In that heat, in the opponent's panic, Storm's coolness and athletic ability serve him well. The athleticism reveals itself most clearly in fencing. "For sheer flexibility," says Micahnik, "he's more loose than most gymnasts. He's very sensitive. He feels he's tight when anyone else would feel they were falling apart."

His legs are thick and muscular. They hurl him forward, pull him backward. "People rarely have enough control to throw their body full speed and still be in command." Storm is speaking, and it is understood without his having said it, that he can do this.

He moves so smoothly! And his body control! How he keeps his upper body independent of the lower, his forearm independent of the shoulder, his wrist independent of the elbow! His body retreats yet attacks, somehow with power in both directions simultaneously. The blade hangs there—a trap—while the rest of his body moves backward. Then Storm suddenly charges with all the fury of a football player on the suicide squad, yet even here he remains in control, continues to maneuver, to dig, to dig, to touch.

"In fencing," he continues, "and in running and swimming, you try to get 'up.' Your blood pressure rises, the veins and arteries dilate, the capillaries open up. They're emotional too. . . .

"The challenge of the pentathlon is that shooting is the opposite. Next to you is a Hungarian. You can't grit your teeth and tell yourself to do better. There must be total calmness, total control."

When Storm shoots he stands casually with one hand in his pocket. One can picture him as a model for *Gentleman's Quarterly*, with a sweater tied about his neck and wearing tassled loafers without socks. He displays quintessential reserve, almost to the point of a seeming ennui. Yet his focus is absolute:

"You know the target is coming seven seconds after the final command. That just adds to the pressure. You have to think only of your sight, not even the target, just your sight. And the gun goes off. You realign the sight, the gun drops, and you forget it. You never move."

"You never move," he repeats. "You bring the gun up a little slow, a little high, jerk the trigger a little, and you drop a place. So the tension would tend to build. That's exactly what you have to repress."

He demonstrates. The gun fires, loudly. Then there is nothing. Just Storm standing there. It is as if everything happened without him, as if he was not involved in the firing of it.

A perfect score in shooting is 200; it has been recorded only twice in major competition, once in 1936 and once in 1978. Storm's best is 195, and he shoots consistently over 190.

The pentathlon is different from other sports. It was designed for army officers at play. The fencing is patterned after how the world works—duels where one touch could mean death. Perhaps the pentathlon really is not a sport at all. Perhaps it was designed as a game of survival in the real world. A microcosm, so to speak. Those who succeed in it will not after retirement make a living from a celebrity status, like a basketball player; they will not sell insurance or open bars. They will succeed in the world, as Storm will.

He does not see the pentathlon as allegory. To him it is a demanding, challenging sport. And, like the others, he wants to be the champion. His obstacle is the last event, the cross-country run. The start is staggered so that if one competitor passes another, he has passed him also in the over-all standings. Storm has been in first and "seen people pass me. It is not a good feeling."

He is standing now in his fraternity library, smiling, animated, with his hands thrust in his pockets. But talking of being passed, the intensity enters his voice. Or an eagerness.

"Everybody thinks, 'We'll give Storm a big lead and catch him in the run.' Well, in Australia nobody caught me."

He is looking forward to 1980.

MARK CAMERON

I t is difficult for an athlete, especially a great athlete, to grow old grace-
fully—to watch helplessly as his reflexes slow, as his strength dete-
riorates, as once-easy feats demand great effort. But Mark Cameron,
five-time national heavyweight weightlifting champion, medal contender
at the Montreal Olympics and bronze medalist in the following year's
world championships, is only 26; the aging process has not yet begun to
sap his abilities. Cameron's problem stems not from growing old but from
something more insidious: growing up.

If the essence of sport is *play*, a reckless pagan exaltation of the physical, if competitive sport also involves going all-out after something,
traditionally, at least, such attitudes are for children. Maturity implies a
willingness to compromise, to accept less than what one wants—or
maybe just distancing oneself from what once seemed such a priority.
Cameron is maturing.

"I'm not starry-eyed anymore," Cameron says. "I've won enough that
winning isn't that important. I've won five straight national championships. What's the big deal in winning six? I used to feel I had something
to prove—that I'm a man, or maybe just that I'm *here*. I don't feel I have
anything left to prove anymore. Now I wouldn't make sacrifices the way
I did before. Every sacrifice I made has hurt me in the end. I'm not going
to sell my soul for an Olympic medal."

If Cameron sounds jaded, even bitter, he is. He literally had his hands
on that Olympic medal: if he had succeeded with his final attempt to lift
490 pounds from the floor to over his head, he would have won the silver. He had lifted that weight just two months earlier to set an American record. But he did not succeed. Yet what made him bitter is that the

failure seemed to turn the establishment of his sport, people he believed were his friends, against him.

Right now he is engaged in a battle to suspend time. He still wants an Olympic medal, but he wants other things, too. He's been married a year and he wants a family life, and a career. He is at a stage past that of Linda Dragan, and is trying simultaneously to hang on and move on.

"I'll postpone things until after the next Olympics," he says, "but after that, lifting can't come first anymore."

It was not always so.

He began lifting for the most trite of reasons: he was small, skinny, and a victim of bullies. He worked hard and discovered he was good. So he lifted more, put in more hours, lifted more weight. He became captain of the track team at Middletown, Rhode Island, High School but wanted to enter a weightlifting meet. So in Boston he competed for the first time and met Joe Mills, a former national champion and coach.

Twice a week Cameron began driving the 100-mile round trip to train with Mills at the Central Falls, Rhode Island, Weightlifting Club. It is no health club. There is no bench for bench presses, no dumbbells, no machines, no lockers, and no mirrors on any wall. A refrigerator holds beer. On the first floor, two lifting platforms fill an area twenty feet wide, facing half a dozen chairs and a refrigerator; in the basement is a shower infested with spiders. In the chairs sit Mills, in his sixties, and former lifters who come to have a beer, socialize, and critique the lifters. But Mills can coach. He developed among others Bob Bednarksi, a world champion and world record holder, Gerry Ferreli, a world teenage record holder, and at least half a dozen junior national champions. As with Cameron, in each of these cases Mills took a young athlete and coached them to success. It is arguably the best club of its kind in the country.

Only competitive Olympic-style lifters train there. Olympic lifting is so named because there is Olympic competition in the sport, and to differentiate it from bodybuilding and power lifting. The sport requires not only raw strength but enormous explosiveness, balance, and skill. It consists of the snatch, when the athlete rips the weight from the floor to over head in one motion, and the clean and jerk, when the athlete pulls the weight from the floor to his shoulders, which is called the "clean," pauses, and then "jerks" the bar over head.

Ramming that weight over head, standing stiff beneath it, a lifter feels absolute control, absolute dominance. It is a magnificent feeling, as triumphant as any in sport.

Cameron was drawn to it. He began a relentless progression of victories: teenage national lightheavyweight champion; the junior national middleheavyweight champion; and the last five years in a row the national heavyweight champion. ABC used films of him to promote the last Olympics, where he finished fifth. A year later he won a bronze medal in the world championships. He has set twenty-seven national records. *Sports Illustrated* profiled him.

"Those days in Central Falls were so fine," Cameron says. "Everything was perfect. My parents were perfect. They were always there helping, but never pushed. Mills is a great coach and I learned a lot, and not just about lifting."

Back then Cameron lived the way he lifted, hard. The first time he attended the national championships, as a teenage spectator, he got to his fourth floor hotel room by climbing the trellis on the outside wall. He started college, dropped out, went back. Summers he worked as a bouncer in Newport bars.

"I used to know the Budweiser label by heart," he jokes. "That used to be an important part of my life."

Then there was the time at a boat show in Boston when he wrestled the bear.

"One of the most vivid images I'll ever have, of anything, was the bear coming across the ring and raising its arms. I just looked *up*. What was I going to do? Put him in a headlock? A bear hug? I lost, but I'd love to wrestle him again. Except for the smell. He stunk. I smelled like a bear for a week."

Cameron could do no wrong back then, back until the Olympics. Back then, he was the fairest of the fair-haired boys.

But there is another side. There is the failure with the 490-pound clean and jerk in the Olympics. There is the fact that since then, he entered graduate school and discovered an excitement about learning. And there is the fact that a year ago he got married.

His life has changed.

At 5′10″ and 234 pounds, Mark Cameron is wide and thick. His muscles have density; his legs, back, shoulders, arms seem dense and heavy beyond statistics. His wife Nina, herself an excellent gymnast with a chance to make an international team, is tiny. Yet she supports him, supports his lifting. Time he spends training does not make her jealous. "Thank God," Cameron jokes.

But the lifting is always present between them, like a guest that has outworn the welcome. Lifting limits the time they share. It is Cameron who complains, "We never see each other," and Cameron who though there are no kids now talks of "family life."

He talks of his work too, his research in biomechanics, the analysis of human motion. His bookshelves are lined with volumes of calculus and physics. He finished his M.A. and says he'd like a Ph.D. His conversation becomes animated as he discusses his work; he attacks his studies the same way he attacks the bar, with a vicious decisiveness. He speaks of "glucocorticoids in the blood…stress reaction…definite psychophysiological connection. My minor is biofeedback." He mentions myoelectrics, attaching electrodes to the body that recognize a pattern of impulses that would normally lead, for example, to clenching a fist; the electrodes, after recognizing the pattern, can then stimulate an artificial limb to do the same thing. It excites him, the way lifting used to.

"I've come a long way from being a phys ed major at URI who drank a lot of beer and wanted to teach high school gym. I want a quality Ph.D. I'll let the academics slide until after the Games, but that's the last time I'll let lifting interfere. I have to take care of my career. I have to take care of my family."

Equally important, lifting isn't play anymore. "I used to love lifting," he says wistfully. "I used to love going to the gym."

Cameron is sitting in his apartment in a graduate student complex at the University of Maryland. He slides a beer from one hand to the other. He looks weary. Talking about the last few years does that to him. His voice is quiet. Trophies and mementoes surround him from all over the world. On one wall hangs an official Olympics flag, a "souvenir."

He begins to talk about his failure with the 490: "I choked all right, but not in the conventional sense. Pressure had an effect on me but it was a long-term thing. I peaked too early. I was burned out. I was always training. Everywhere I went people were calling me America's only hope. I was always going, going, going. I thought I couldn't take time off. I thought I could always rest *after* the Olympics. It just burned me out. The last two weeks I didn't care anymore. We lifted at the end of the Games. I just wanted to get it over with.

"As I was going out for the 490 I kept thinking, 'Well it's finally over.' I tried to fight that off but it kept coming back." He shakes his head. "It kept coming back."

He had lifted that same weight so effortlessly three months earlier at the national championships. An American record. Now, for the silver medal. . . . He missed it badly.

"I went out to dinner that night with a friend. He told me I looked twelve years younger than that afternoon. My response to the miss was disgust. I didn't get crushed until later. It was like I had to rest up to get crushed."

There were other blows, and each one took more and more fun out of the sport. Not only had he failed, but another American, Lee James, surprised the world and took a silver medal in a lighter class. Cameron's foibles, particularly his abrasive manner around the lifting platform— "granted I've been arrogant," he says—were no longer tolerated. Lee James became the fair-haired boy and Cameron now admits, "I was jealous. We didn't get along and it was my fault. As soon as I realized that, I was ashamed of myself and went to talk to him. We get along fine now."

But there are others with whom Cameron no longer gets along. In the World Championships the year after the Olympics he did win a bronze medal. But last year the World Championships were held in Gettysburg, Pennsylvania. Cameron, ill at the time, did not compete. Members of the weightlifting establishment—Karl Miller, a former national coach, Adam Swirz, member of several committees, and others—refused even to talk to him when he arrived to watch. They implied he wasn't really sick. They "as much as called me a liar." Miller told a lifting publication that he wanted no part of those who "gave less than their best," and it was clear whom Miller was accusing.

"That hurt," Cameron says. "I thought these people were my *friends*. Oh it hurt. How could they question my integrity? Why? The World

Championships in the United States? My friends, family, everybody was going! I trained ten months for that one meet, and I was leaving with a medal, *period.*" Even now he seems puzzled by what happened, and bitter. "Adam Swirz—he was at the first meet I ever went to. How many beers have I had with that guy?"

"I'll tell you one thing. I found out who my real friends are. Like Joe Mills always said, 'God protect me from my friends. I can protect myself from my enemies.'"

A wife, disenchantment with lifting, a nascent career all push Cameron away from the weightlifting bar. He no longer lives solely for the moments on the platform, just he and the bar and the admiring audience.

So why lift at all?

Dick Smith, manager of the 1980 Olympic lifting team, insists Cameron still has "more potential than anyone in the country. He has the ability to do great things."

But fulfilling his potential no longer interests Cameron. He says he has nothing left to prove. He wants to return to the Olympics for two reasons.

"The games are special," he says. "I think they are sacred. That may sound naive, but I really do. It's not what the media and officials make of them—that's not real games. It's the other athletes, eating with them, meeting them. I don't see it as a competition against other athletes, but against myself."

And he wants to finish what he left incomplete in the last Games. That's all. He says if he had won the medal then, he wouldn't be lifting now.

Weights are everywhere in this gym near the University of Maryland. The clank of plates and the grunts of effort punctuate the silence. This gym is a collection of egotists; each person is entirely into himself, and it is entirely unlike Central Falls where Cameron started. Here are bodybuilders, power lifters, and Cameron. Here no one watches anyone else lift regardless of how much weight is on the bar; to interrupt one's own workout to watch would be admitting someone else is better.

But when Cameron lifts, everyone only pretends not to watch, pretends not to be impressed, pretends not to notice. Each has noticed. And not just the weight.

A tension erupts when Cameron steps on the platform. The way he stalks the bar communicates his intensity. Even with a light weight with which he drills on technique—light for him anyway; it is 253 pounds— there is a dynamism. He chalks his hands, places his hands on the bar, rotates his grip until it feels right.... "*YAAAHHHH!*" The bar explodes overhead! "*YAAAHHHH!*" again! "*YAAAHHHH!*" again! Each complete lift finished in less than second!

Now he takes deep breaths and sits on the edge of the raised platform, alone. He takes his blood pressure; he takes it several times a day and believes it measures overtraining. He will never overtrain again, never burn himself out again.

A powerlifter asks advice.

Cameron gives it. The other lifter wants to discuss it. Cameron snaps, "You asked. I told you. *Don't* do what I say. See if I care."

He turns his back, back to the bar for his next lift. That is the old Cameron, arrogant, intolerant. The champion Cameron, which he is trying to recapture.

It is difficult, once the element of play has gone and once the emotional need to win has evaporated, to compete successfully with the best in the world. But Cameron points out that three months ago he set his first personal—and national—record since the last Olympics, and he tied another personal and national record in winning his fifth national championship one month ago. He insists his lifts have started to move again. He is brusque, confident: "I'm not going to school this next year. I'll have very few distractions. I'm right on schedule."

He plans finally to get it over with. And then, move on.

POSTSCRIPT

The 1980 Olympic Games were held in Moscow.
In 1979, the Soviet Union invaded Afghanistan. It was an invasion which would have tremendous consequences. President Jimmy Carter ordered American athletes to boycott those games. All the energy, all the focus, all the hope and a significant portion of the lives of each of these athletes and hundreds more was wasted. And in 1989 the Soviets boycotted the Los Angeles games.

The Olympics are supposed to be beyond politics, but that was never true. Issues of race and class—gentlemen of leisure and ladies of that class being the only ones who could truly afford amateur status—have always pervaded the games.

Boycotting the Olympics was hardly the only response to the invasion by the U.S. government. Carter also forbade the shipment of grains to the Soviets. More importantly, the Reagan administration funded and helped create the Afghan resistance to the Soviet invasion. That resistance was led by Islamic extremists—violent extremists, who after the collapse of the Soviet Union targeted the United States.

THE FALL

I t is said that politics is a contact sport. Gingrich played that sport bru-
tally, just short of war, breaking unwritten rules, creating a new model
of behavior. He had worried that if Wright survived the attack "he
could be the greatest Speaker since Henry Clay." Gingrich intended to do
everything in his power to prevent Wright's survival.

Wright had played hard as well. One of his aides had said the way to
handle Gingrich was "to gut him and leave him hanging out there for everyone to see." But no one, including the man who spoke those words, had
tried to do that. All of Wright's energies and all the energies of his staff and
allies had gone to advancing his policy agenda, and he had used his power
ruthlessly. He had broken unwritten rules, too. In so doing he had played
into Gingrich's hands.

For Gingrich, his pounding and pounding on Wright's ethics paid off. His
campaign did not die; it came together. The media did take off on it, and,
once started, the process had to work itself to its end. The end was not inevitable, but some great explosion was.

On another note, allow me to explain my methodology. This section in-
cludes quotations from executive sessions of the Ethics Committee. Unlike
most of the other quotations in this book, I was of course not present when
these statements were made. But all quotes from Ethics Committee deliberations come from a transcript of the executive session. Leaks served me
well, too. I might add that I offered these transcripts to any reporter covering the events. They are still available. Not a single reporter has ever sought
access to them.

THE TRIAL

The House Ethics Committee, officially the Committee on Standards and Official Conduct, served as investigator, prosecutor, grand jury, jury, judge, and appeals court. And although the full House technically acted as Supreme Court, it has never over-ruled the committee. All of the important phases were conducted in executive session—in secret. Committee rules allowed it to "adopt special procedures deemed necessary to a particular matter." In other words, there were no rules. The United States was said to be a government of law and not men; the Ethics Committee exercised power through men and not law. The House had given the committee such power and flexibility so it could protect members. The presumption had always been that it would do so. But investigating the Speaker of the House, particularly this Speaker, altered the presumptions.

The committee chairman was Julian Dixon. He was a strong chairman. If he chose to be. The media would scrutinize every action of the committee. One of Dixon's closest intimates warned John Mack, "If you want to understand what drives Julian, read the morning papers." There was something else. Wright's attorney Bill Oldaker was close to Dixon. Not far into the process Dixon pulled him aside. "How long do you think Jim plans to be Speaker," Dixon asked. "I'm not sure Jim's the right person to be Speaker at this time."

And there was one other thing. This committee was the only one in the entire Congress equally divided between Democrats and Republicans.

Gingrich did not hesitate to send committee Republicans memos on strategy. The media pressure on all members of the committee was far greater. The Republicans' active hatred of Wright, the Democrats' lukewarm loyalty to him, and the press made the Republicans more than equal.

And here, ranking Republican John Myers drove the process. Dixon allowed him to. It was chiefly Myers who was responsible for hiring Richard Phelan as outside counsel. As Myers later explained approvingly, "I heard he was *very* ambitious."

Ambitious indeed. Although no one knew it at the time, Phelan planned to run for governor of Illinois. He knew the investigation would generate immense publicity, and, if he brought Wright down, it would cast him as a reformer taking on the most powerful leader of his own party. It would be a grand stepping-stone in Chicago, where the Democratic machine was considered corrupt.

Tall and thin, at fifty-two Phelan still had a Huck Finn look that came from a lock of hair that regularly fell onto his forehead. He had founded and built a sixty-lawyer firm dedicated to litigation. But he had grown bored litigating. A few months before he sought the job as outside counsel, he had decided to take a sabbatical from the firm he had founded. He had money; after the investigation finished he explored running for governor immediately but put that move off to the future, first spending $850,000 of his own money to win a county elective office to strengthen his position for the later gubernatorial run. A magazine profile described him as "supremely egotistical," as someone who "likes to throw out theories—occasionally wild ones—while associates search for case law to support them."

As the outside counsel investigating Wright, he would step into the most exciting arena he had ever played in. In a superficial sense he understood the stakes, but only as they affected him, and he was unaware of the rumblings of deeper things. He was like a small boy sitting on his father's lap with his hands on a steering wheel, thinking he was driving the car. The members were shrewder than he: not more intelligent, but shrewder about the world, with a deeper understanding of it and of the use of things. One member went so far as to say, "Phelan was frankly naive."

But the process gave him extraordinary power and he was not naive about how to use it.

Dixon and Myers let him. For example, committee rules required exculpatory material to be immediately given to the respondent; Phelan accumulated thousands of pages of evidence, but never turned over a single page to Wright's attorney Bill Oldaker. He was waiting for Dixon to force him to. Dixon never did.

The first stage of the proceeding was Phelan's investigation and taking of testimony. Members of the committee were welcome to sit in when witnesses testified, but almost never did more than two appear. They were busy men. Not a single member of the committee actually heard all the witnesses. The committee would rely on Phelan's report for its facts. No representative of Wright was allowed to be present to hear, much less cross-examine, a single witness. If Phelan truly was impartial this made little difference, but if he played the role of a prosecutor, if he carefully selected the evidence he presented, no one would be able to rebut him. Only Phelan would know the facts.

Wright had done some things that needed explanation under any standard. Phelan accepted no explanations, for anything.

After eight months, Phelan delivered a 476-page report. In it he charged Wright with 117 violations of House rules. If Phelan's report was a fair, impartial representation of the truth, then Jim Wright would be driven from his speakership in deserved disgrace.

In the report, Phelan painted a portrait of greed and corruption, even if doing so required distortions: misstating a crucial date; dismissing one witness's testimony as hearsay when it was not; saying it "is reasonable to assume" that a Wright aide did something which she had not done, then stating it as a fact. Each of these distortions was seemingly insignificant or accidental, but all of them pointed in one direction—toward Wright's guilt. And cumulatively they appeared to have weight.

More significantly, on point after point after point, Phelan simply ignored all evidence or testimony which exonerated Wright, and presented as fact testimony, even when contradicted by other evidence, which condemned him. Sometimes he not only ignored testimony but distorted it, usually by using half-truths, but occasionally with a flat lie. Some examples:

...Phelan charged that in a meeting with savings and loan regulators "Wright made it plain that he...was not simply seeking impartial consideration of [Thomas] Gaubert's claim, but a change in the Bank Board's regulatory response to Gaubert. Such use of Wright's influence is a violation of House Rule XLIII, clause 1."

Eight people attended that meeting. One witness who had no connection to Wright and at least three other witnesses—and possibly more—testified that neither Gaubert's name nor his situation was even mentioned at that meeting, and no such pressure was exerted. Even if one or more witnesses had testified otherwise—and only Phelan knew if anyone actually made that accusation—a fair presentation would have cited conflicting testimony. Phelan simply rejected all testimony which contradicted his charge.

. . . Nearly all of Phelan's charges against Wright involved his relationship with his friend and business partner George Mallick. Together they had formed an investment company called Mallightco, each of them putting in an identical amount of capital so they were equal partners.

Yet when the partners bought $40,000 worth of stock on margin together, Phelan argued that this amounted to a gift to Wright of Mallick's credit: "I submit to you that [Wright] probably could not have bought margin stock on that basis without the credit of someone else."

This was an absurd statement. Virtually anyone can buy on margin. Someone who buys a stock on margin pays half the purchase price in cash; the broker keeps the stock itself as collateral. If the price of the stock falls, the buyer either pays more money or the broker sells the stock.

. . . Phelan charged Wright with accepting $5,000 in unreported and illegal gifts from Mallick in the form of reduced interest. He claimed that Mallick had borrowed $150,000 and then loaned it to Wright at 3.5 percent less.

This charge was an outright lie. In fact, Mallick had taken out an adjustable rate loan for $150,000 at 13.5 percent. He kept half, and loaned half—not all of it—to the Wrights, who paid him a *fixed* rate of 13.5 percent.

When interest rates rose, Mallick did pay as high as 17 percent on the total loan, while Wright continued to pay 13.5 percent. Over the first two and a half years of the loan, this meant that Wright did in effect receive a $5,000 subsidy from the Mallicks. But the loan lasted eight years; for the next five and a half years, as interest rates fell to 7.5 percent, Wright's fixed rate almost doubled what Mallick paid. Over the length of the loan, Wright paid more in total interest than did Mallick. Far from giving Wright a gift, Mallick profited on the loan to Wright. Phelan omitted any mention of this fact. He simply stopped calculating the "gift" when market rates dropped below 13.5 percent.

Phelan's report was filled with this kind of illogic. But only someone who knew the facts understood how weak the report was. And the press would read only Phelan's version of it, completely unrebutted. That was certain. Dixon and Myers had decided that as soon as the committee took formal action they would release the report to the press.

Wright would have no opportunity to rebut it. He would not see the report until after its release.

For weeks, members of the committee read Phelan's report in private and leaked the most damaging tidbits to the press. The press would measure the performance of committee members, especially Democrats, against these leaks.

How could they justify not voting against Wright? They could not charge partisanship. Phelan had been selected as a delegate to the Democratic national convention. Republicans and Phelan's report placed their integrity and the integrity of the House at issue. They needed reasons to support Wright. Very good reasons.

If the committee found "reason to believe"—that was the standard of proof—that Wright had violated any House rules, it would issue a "statement of alleged violations," in effect an indictment. Then would come the "disciplinary hearing," a public trial in which the standard of proof rose to "clear and convincing evidence." That would be followed, if he was found guilty, by a hearing on sanctions. But there were never public trials. The statement of alleged violations had always effectively ended the proceedings and were accepted by the defendants, although they sometimes disputed the sanctions on the House floor—and always lost.

Wright's attorney Oldaker asked Dixon for a chance to rebut Phelan's oral presentation. Dixon agreed. But he would not allow Oldaker to read Phelan's report. Or see the evidence on which the charges were based. Or contact the witnesses for information about their testimony. Or present any evidence. Oldaker's only knowledge of Phelan's case would come from the notes he took of Phelan's oral argument.

On February 27, 1989, the committee convened in executive session in an empty Rayburn Building hearing room. Outside in the hall, reporters lounged about, made jokes, and waited for anyone to emerge to give them some hint of the proceedings. Inside, the twelve members sat at a raised dais. Before them, where witnesses usually testified, was a podium with a microphone, which separated Phelan and Oldaker. They sat twenty-four inches apart, flanked by assistants at long tables. The rows of chairs, normally filled at committee hearings, were empty. The two tables reserved for the press were empty. There were only the members, the attorneys, and the microphone.

Phelan would go first, speak for several days, and be questioned by members, while Oldaker remained silent. Then Oldaker would speak, followed by Phelan's rebuttal. The arguments would last until March 14. After they ended, Oldaker would play no further role in the deliberations. Phelan would continue to be part of the proceedings, continue to answer members' questions about the testimony.

Phelan began his attack. The members were tense, quiet, listening. There were two keys to his charges. The first involved Mallightco, the Wright-Mallick partnership. Wright's wife Betty had been working directly for Mallick part-time for an $18,000 salary and a rent-free apartment that Wright used when home in Fort Worth. (Mallick also gave other employees, including his lawyer, rent-free apartments.) After Mallightco was formed, she switched payrolls from Mallick to Mallightco at the same salary and benefits and began looking for investment opportunities. The company began with $116,000 in capital, half from Mallick, half from Wright. In two years its value almost quadrupled, to over $400,000.

But in his oral presentation, Phelan called the company "an artifice, a sham, a conduit to provide the Speaker and his wife with cash dividends and salaries and apartments and condominiums and loans, all in violation of the rules of this House of Representatives." He argued that Betty's job was also a sham, that she did not work: "This is a case of a person who is on a payroll who isn't doing anything...a ghost payroller.... This person, as far as we can see, did absolutely no work whatsoever and played no role.... Over the course of some ten years some $160,000 worth of gifts were funneled through this corporation to the Wrights."

Betty Wright's job was supposedly to look for investment opportunities. But Phelan said, "I asked [Mallick's assistant] Pamela Smith how much time Mrs. Wright spent over the four years she worked at Mallightco.... She answered... perhaps a dozen days over four years [was] Betty Wright working on clearly identifiable projects."

And again: "The best you can say is that for a dozen days over four years she supposedly worked on some clearly identified projects. Is twelve days' worth of work worth $72,000? And we are not talking about a [merger and acquisition] person in New York....

"We concluded that there was no evidence to show that there was any benefit conferred on Mallightco of whatever value by Mrs. Wright.... [Her] salary was a downright, outright gift paid through Mallightco to the Wrights... they were not reported, they were from someone with a direct interest in legislation, made to James C. Wright Jr."

But Phelan was distorting the testimony again. He had asked Pamela Smith, "Can you give the chairman of the committee how much time that Mrs. Wright may have spent... Hours? Days? Weeks? Months?"

Smith had replied, "On an average month we would see Mrs. Wright five to seven days a month, and she would be in our offices [in Fort Worth] working." She added that Mrs. Wright also did work for the company in Washington and New York. Smith then cited several specific examples of projects she had worked on.

Phelan had taken the specific examples, credited each with a few days work, added them up, and then charged that Betty Wright had worked only a "dozen days" on "identifiable projects."

He could never have made such a distortion in a courtroom where actual witnesses testified, and where the defense could put on a case.

But he could make it here, in an executive session of a Congressional committee, knowing that a press firestorm would erupt the instant the committee charged Wright with anything—a firestorm likely to force a resignation long before any public hearing of evidence occurred.

When it came time for questions, Democrats objected angrily. Alan Mollohan, his tone sarcastic but intense, concerned, asked, "You would suggest that Mr. Mallick was laying a groundwork for some unspecified, unknown relationship in the future?"

"Yes sir."

"But you didn't have any facts to substantiate that, did you?"

"Well, I don't know what would be more important to a real estate developer in Fort Worth, to his future—"

"You didn't have any information to suggest his past relationship was anticipating any specific legislative interest, did you?"

"Neither he nor any of the other witnesses said that they were giving gifts in order that Speaker Wright would be our prisoner futurely, no."

Even some Republicans were troubled by Phelan's argument. Thomas Petri asked, "Was there any evidence that Mallick actually ever got anything specific of a monetary value from the federal government?"

Phelan: "We didn't find that he had economically benefitted. . . . [But] it offended me. To suggest that Mallick did it because he was a good guy and Wright was his best friend—this is a tough, hardnosed businessman. I have to presume and assume that he certainly assumed he would economically benefit."

Back to the Democrats with Vic Fazio: "Other characters who have come before this committee, there has always been a quid pro quo. Not only is there no quid pro quo, there apparently isn't any effort on Mallick's part that would have brought a quid pro quo."

Phelan conceded, "There isn't any quid pro quo."

Joe Gaydos had another problem. Betty Wright had worked directly for Mallick in 1979 and 1980. Phelan conceded that she had done real work then. Gaydos noted, "Here is a woman employed by Mallick and no questions are asked, she transfers to a new corporation, and she is then supposed to be in a position whereby she is getting paid for doing absolutely nothing. Why bother to transfer her?"

That bothered Chester Atkins too: "You ascribe her first job [with] Mallick as bona fide employment. In her second job with Mallightco you suggest that it was not bona fide and you ascribe 100 percent of it as a gift. Do you think that is fair in light of the fact that she did appear to have done work?"

Indeed, since Wright owned half of Mallightco he paid half Betty's salary. If she added no value then transferring her from Mallick's own company—where even Phelan agreed she had done real work—to the partnership in effect cut her pay 50 percent. Her salary had to be paid from dividends Wright would have otherwise collected.

As Democrats questioned Phelan, he banged his fist against the podium. His voice rose with conviction. His finger jabbed the air. It was his jury performance. But he never grew angry, never offended, always mixed argument with unction. When Fazio probed him, Phelan said, "That's an excellent question! You would have made a hell of a lawyer, Mr. Fazio!" With Gaydos, who like Phelan went to Notre Dame, Phelan joked, "We're Number One, right?"

Phelan's deputy Michael Howlett Jr., whom Phelan had brought with him from Chicago, ran into a Chicago business executive, shook his head in disgust, and said, "We're doing a dirty thing here."

The next day Phelan moved to the book. It was Wright's weakest moral position, although his defense on technical grounds looked strong. Wright was supposed to receive 55 percent in royalties (as it turned out, his publisher never paid him much of the royalties he had earned), far higher than the industry standard of 15 percent. Most books were sold to bulk purchasers, several of whom were lobbyists. Without question, Wright had exploited his office for personal gain.

Yet House rules specifically exempted royalties from income limitations. The book was entirely within the rules. Wright had gotten legal advice confirming that. Other members of Congress had written books, although usually for mainstream publishers, and lobbyists routinely bought large quantities. No one had ever questioned them. Wright had exploited a loophole, yes. It was a major embarrassment, yes, and raised real questions about his judgement and even his ethics. But it did not violate the rules.

The committee had asked Phelan to investigate only whether the book had served as a vehicle to transfer campaign funds to personal use. The trail of money was clear and no such transfer had happened, yet rather than exonerate Wright, Phelan left a shadow over him, saying, "When looking at the original charge . . . we remain unable to prove or disprove [it.]"

And Phelan made other charges, searching for a way around the House rules. First, although Wright had written—not had ghostwritten—three other books published by mainstream publishers, and had written for such magazines as *Harper's*, Phelan argued that his book was not really a book, and that his royalties were profits from a business venture. That meant that 100 percent of the income violated House limits on outside earnings. To make his case, he argued that Wright's 55 percent royalty was totally unique. But another publisher had testified that he had offered Wright a 50 percent royalty. Phelan told the committee that this offer had been 25 percent. When Phelan said that he told a flat lie.

He also argued that Wright used the book to violate outside earnings limits by converting honoraria, which were legal but limited to a total of $30,000 a year, to royalties.

As Phelan went through his arguments, reviewing bulk book purchases which seemed connected to speeches, he quoted Gerald Cassidy, a lobbyist. Oldaker sat up. Although he had never seen Cassidy's testimony, he was certain Phelan was lying about it.

Oldaker was not allowed to interrupt Phelan or object to anything he said. But as the committee was about to recess, he raised a "point of inquiry" and asked to be allowed to review the deposition. It was his first complaint in two days of listening to Phelan.

Dixon rejected Oldaker's request, saying that if the committee later charged Wright he could see it then.

Then he turned to his colleagues and said, "I would say to each member of the committee, we should look at our report to see if in fact the statements that are made are correct."

He was ruling that Phelan's report—not the actual testimony—be used to check Phelan's accuracy, when that accuracy was being questioned.

But one Republican, James Hansen, did check the original sources on another charge, that Wright had failed to report certain items on his disclosure forms. Hansen complained to Phelan, "Contrary to the impression I got, this was reported." Then Hansen asked about other similar benefits: "You mentioned yesterday [these] were not reported?"

"That's correct," Phelan replied. "They were not reported."

But they had been reported. Phelan had lied, gotten caught, then told the same lie again.

Why did the committee trust him? Or didn't they trust him? Were they just using him? Were they just asking for reasons before they voted?

A lobbyist explained in another context—but one which applied here as well—"Sometimes you'll talk to a member and he'll say, 'Give me your arguments.' That usually means he'll vote with you. You never know why. Maybe it's because of a contribution. He can't tell the press that. When he asks for your arguments, he's asking for reasons to justify his vote."

Reasons are both weapons and armor. They do not necessarily convince, but they can be used to attack and defend. Phelan was giving Republicans reasons to justify voting against Wright.

Finally came the savings and loans. They would spend most of the day on it. Wright's involvement over a particular savings and loan had sparked Jack Anderson columns, *Newsweek* stories, the *Regardie's* story, and had sparked much of Gingrich's entire campaign.

Phelan said about the savings and loan issue, "We don't find probably any problem."

The irony.

Even so, Phelan charged Wright with using "undue influence" on four other occasions with industry regulators. Phelan had no evidence that Wright had acted improperly. So he reversed the argument, said that Wright's actions and intent were irrelevant, and that the sole judges of whether Wright was exercising undue influence were the regulators themselves. He insisted, "The point is, what is in the minds of those persons at the Bank Board? Whether they were reasonable in their assumptions, whether they were correct in their assumptions, I don't think is an issue. Right or wrong, reasonable or unreasonable, that is what they acted on and that is what they did."

Again: "Whether it is true or not, it doesn't make any difference. It is what is the impression given the agency."

Phelan was holding Wright accountable not for his actions, not even for his intentions, but for what someone else thought were his intentions.

Yet Myers said, "What other standard would you use?"

And Republican Thomas Petri observed, "The savings and loan scandal is an enormous one.... This is going at some point to be in the public arena. It is going to be reviewed and discussed. Not only the Speaker's performance—our performance."

Petri wanted a scapegoat. The press was watching. The press was a driving force even inside an executive session of this Ethics Committee.

Phelan had finished.

Finally it was Oldaker's turn. According to a study by the University of Chicago law school, in 75 percent of cases the single most important part of a trial is the opening statement. Oldaker began:

"I need not tell you that you have in your hands the life of Jim Wright. What you decide could well make a determination as to how history is going to view this man. This man has served his country as a public servant for forty years. He volunteered for the service the day after Pearl Harbor. He was elected to Congress in 1954, at the age of thirty-one, and has been reelected seventeen times, six times unopposed. In 1987, as you all know, he became Speaker. There is not a blemish on his record. And there is not one allegation in this entire case that he broke the law. He is not accused anywhere of perjury, bribery, or any of the other pernicious acts that bring congressmen down."

The members stirred. It sounded as if Oldaker was saying let Wright off because he was Speaker, that he had done nothing really so bad.

Oldaker next complained that Phelan had broadened the investigation far beyond the original charges: "I thought that this committee would not go on fishing expeditions. Suddenly all of Jim Wright's entire life back to 1949 was an issue."

Members stirred again. Was he saying that Phelan had found something but it shouldn't count because he shouldn't have looked?

Finally, Oldaker talked about gifts: "We have two types of gifts...benign gifts.... You could accept those benign gifts in any amount of money, without limit. Then there are pernicious gifts, from lobbyists, foreign agents, people who have a direct interest in legislation.... If Mr. Mallick doesn't have a direct interest in legislation, what we are talking about is moving all of the things that were disclosed by Mr. Wright on [his financial disclosure] form from one place to another. Mrs. Wright's salary. Disclosed? Yes. It is on the form. It is disclosed. We think she was paid a legitimate amount of money.... For assumption's sake, credit Mr. Phelan, you move salary to gift. The public knows the same thing, right?"

Democrat Vic Fazio listened intently and later said, "Oldaker seemed to be conceding Phelan's facts—that Betty hadn't worked."

And contrary to Oldaker's claim, disclosing $100,000 as salary when it really is a gift does not tell the public the same thing. Not the same thing at all. His own point about disclosure devastated him. One member looked at Phelan and saw him smiling.

Oldaker was treating this case as though Wright were an average member. He was making a cozy argument, insider to insider. His argument could not withstand media scrutiny. Every member recognized how intense the media coverage would be. Oldaker did not. It was not Phelan the outsider who was naive, but Oldaker.

Later he did quote Pamela Smith's testimony that Betty had worked "five to seven days a month," contradicting Phelan. But he never played impresario, never painted a benign portrait of Mallightco, never insisted fiercely that Betty Wright had worked. His defense rested not on the facts but on rules of evidence and logic. Legally he was on unassailable ground. He cited a Supreme Court decision supporting him. Chip Pashayan, a Republican, read it overnight and told him, "You're right."

But this was not a group of judges reviewing legal briefs. This was a jury, a jury of politicians with their own agendas and their own interests at stake.

It was over.

The Ethics Committee dismissed every single charge that had been raised either by Common Cause or by Gingrich. Every one.

But Phelan had made new charges. And the committee was accepting some of them.

Wright asked to testify again. Committee rules stipulate that the accused has a right to respond to charges against him. None of these new charges had existed when he testified before. He had never addressed any of them. He had never been asked about them. *No one* had been asked about them.

The committee refused to allow him to testify.

The Republicans were a block. They had waited a long time for power. Thirty-four years had passed since they had had a voice in who would be

Speaker. All six were voting against Wright. If any Democrat wavered, Wright was lost. And there were so many charges. There was just so much. In isolation, each was easy to dismiss. But all of them? And who on the committee fought for Wright, pulled colleagues aside for him, called Phelan a liar for him? Maybe Mollohan. But he got so frustrated he walked out half the time.

On the book charges, the committee voted that seven times in three years Wright had improperly used book sales to evade the limit on honoraria. But even if the committee was correct, Wright would have made only $4,500 from these transactions, just $1,500 a year. That hardly seemed enough to destroy a speakership.

Then came the issue of Betty's work.

Pashayan reiterated the standard of proof: *reason to believe.*

By a vote of 10–2, the committee decided that there was reason to believe that Betty Wright did no work. In total, it charged that her salary and benefits amounted to $145,000 in gifts. (Logic failed in the amount: the committee judged all her pay and benefits a gift from Mallick, but Wright owned half the partnership and thus paid half his wife's salary and benefits.) $145,000. That was a number that would resonate with the press and public.

The room fell silent.

One member of the committee sat thinking, *Jim Wright can not survive this. Not this.*

Dixon and Myers decided to charge Wright with sixty-nine violations of House rules—seven for the book, sixty-two related to Betty's job. The full committee did not discuss the decision to charge sixty-nine violations, but Myers later said, "It was discussed by the chairman, myself, and Phelan. We were aware of the impact it would have."

On Friday, April 14, Wright walked through the reception area outside his office into an aide's office, where Oldaker was.

"They say the committee is charging me with violating House rules sixty-nine times," Wright said softly. "That's not true is it, Bill?"

"I'm afraid it is, Mr. Speaker."

Wright was very still for a moment. Then, silently, he walked back past his aide's secretary, past the reception area, past his own secretary, and sat down at his desk. *All his years of service. For what? For what? For what?*

On Sunday, April 16, the committee delivered to Jim Wright a statement of his alleged violations.

Wright wanted a trial, as soon as possible. The committee wouldn't give him one, wouldn't even set a date. Dixon and Myers justified that because, they told a huge media audience, Phelan was still investigating Mallightco's purchase of a "nearly worthless" oilwell for $9,000 which was sold the same day for $440,000. That kind of profit would definitely resonate with the media and the public and guaranteed that the story would continue.

The press began to devour Jim Wright.

Wright released affidavits from outsiders proving that Betty had worked. Most reporters who saw the affidavits recognized how weak the charge was, but no national publication investigated and declared his likely innocence on this, and most stories continued to repeat the charge. Only the Fort Worth paper, which had been among the most aggressive in investigating Wright, did a story. Its reporter Ron Hutcheson concluded, "I'm convinced Betty worked. It's not even an issue with me."

The press shifted to other issues. The most important seemed the still-unsettled oil well deal, which the *Wall Street Journal* called "potentially more serious" than anything with which the committee had yet charged Wright. And the *New York Times* and the *Journal* competed to "move" that story, to hunt down each thread to a conclusion. They investigated campaign contributions from other investors in the project. They elaborated on Wright's past favors for Texas oil interests. But they did not investigate the charge itself.

Two papers did. Babcock, the *Washington Post* investigative reporter who broke the stories on Wright's book, wrote the first, and a team of reporters at the *Fort Worth Star-Telegram* published their findings in a special section. Both newspapers agreed: Phelan had mischaracterized the deal; there was nothing wrong with it.

Mallightco had actually committed not $9,000 but $99,000 to the project—$9,000 for mineral rights, $90,000 for its share of drilling an exploratory well. The well found reserves worth $80 to $120 million. The holding shot up in value. Mallightco sold part of its interest for $440,000. But before it could transfer title, it first had to pay off all its creditors; it bought and sold the well in one day no more than any homeowner who pays off his mortgage with the proceeds of a house sale before title transfer. Phelan had lied again.

Babcock's story did not run on the front page of the *Post*; it was buried inside. Even other *Post* reporters ignored it. The Fort Worth paper's special section went unread or ignored by the national media.

Instead, *after* both stories ran, the *New York Times* front page blared, "Profits from Dry Well Pose Tough Questions for Wright." A subheadline announced: "The property was sold for a one day profit of nearly 4,000 percent."

The pack had a direction. It would not be deterred.

The media ignored other factual problems with Phelan and the committee action. Democratic Congressman David Obey, well known as a leader in ethics, had chaired the committee which wrote the House rules on royalty income, and he publicly accused the committee of misapplying House rules. Harold Sawyer, a former Republican congressman who also helped write those rules, excoriated Phelan's legal reasoning, stated that Wright broke no rules, and concluded that "any qualified lawyer" would have advised him that his book transactions were allowed.

All the press had this information. Not a single reporter printed any reference to it.

Another issue: Gene Payte had testified before the committee, and Phelan's report lied about his testimony, completely reversing what he had said.

Payte reacted with outrage, and issued an affidavit correcting this.

Dixon and Myers promptly threatened to find him in contempt of Congress if he continued to make public comments about his testimony—even though it was being mischaracterized—because it had been given in executive session. They also wrote a letter to every witness before the committee threatening anyone who discussed his or her testimony with a contempt of Congress citation. The vast majority of witnesses were part of the Washington community in some way; many of them were lobbyists. Almost half the committee, including both Dixon and Myers, were senior members of the Appropriations Committee. No one in the Washington community would risk a career by antagonizing them.

Despite efforts by Wright's office to publicize both Payte's correction and the committee's attempt to suppress it and intimidate other witnesses, not a newspaper in the country ran a story on the subject.

Richard Dunham of the *Dallas Times-Herald* did write a page-one story detailing some of the attacks on Phelan's report. "It was a pretty lonely feeling out there," Dunham said. "No one else was doing it. We did positive stories and negative stories. The negative ones were picked up by AP. The positive ones died."

"There is a tendency to move in a herd," said Thomas Kenworthy, the *Post*'s lead House reporter. He knew of several discrepancies in Phelan's report, and said, "I thought about investigating the report, but the committee seems to have faith in it. What's Phelan's motive to screw Wright? Why would the Democrats on the committee go along?"

But his most important reason for not examining Phelan's accuracy was the process: "The story's very competitive. It's intense. None of us likes to get beat. If someone's driving this story, it would be Al Hunt."

Hunt was bureau chief of the *Wall Street Journal*. Kenworthy would not take time away from looking for conflicts of interest in Wright's legislative history, or covering Wright's chances for survival for fear of being beaten. And the *Journal* was on this story. Brooks Jackson could already claim credit for St. Germain's election defeat, and now he focused on Wright's activities outside Congress. Jackson judged some of what Wright had done harshly, saying, "That is not appropriate behavior. . . . If I'm harder on him than other reporters, so be it."

David Rogers, the *Journal*'s chief congressional reporter, drove the stories on Wright's legislative history. He was spending hours reviewing it. On one issue he knew something about he said, "I was unimpressed with Phelan's work." But he never questioned Phelan's accuracy because, "I always thought [the case] would go to trial and balance out. . . . Phelan wasn't available. You couldn't ask him how come he was so sloppy with the interest rate thing. It was daily journalism. You couldn't get a quote. Wright was much more exposed to reporters' questions. . . .

[And] I didn't feel I had the time to go off and do a thorough piece on other things. We had to stay competitive. I felt I had to keep up with everyone else."

As James Doyle, once the chief political correspondent for *Newsweek*, had observed, "Your editor sees the AP lead, the *Washington Post* lead, the *New York Times* lead. You have to have great willpower and self-assurance to go in a different direction."

There was another thing. Rogers said, "It frustrated me that Phelan didn't tighten his case more. My role almost was to tighten his case for him.... It was the natural role for a reporter."

Was it personal? Perhaps there need not be anything personal. Perhaps Rogers was right: it was natural for reporters to attack. The process itself, the forces within the press, were inexorable enough. An Ethics Committee Republican watched the press swirl about Wright and observed, "Editors are assigning reporters and giving them budgets, and reporters want Pulitzer Prizes."

A fury was out there. The press had a direction. It would accept no other.

Canetti: *They are not a multitude and have to make up in intensity what they lack in actual numbers.... The truest and most natural pack is that from which our word derives, the hunting pack.... [It] is out for killing and it knows whom it wants to kill.... The proclaiming of the goal...is enough to make the crowd form. This concentration on killing is of a special kind and of unsurpassed intensity. Everyone wants to participate, everyone strikes a blow.*

Republicans gave no quarter. *They're not colleagues*, Cheney had said. *There's no comity left.* One of Wright's few GOP friends said, "I'd like to help Jim. I think awfully well of him. But the pressure is just too much. The big thing is, if the Democrats can stay united, they can win this thing."

Democrats were not united. Politics has always been cold, colder than other professions perhaps. But it had also been intimate. Brutus had stood as close to Caesar as a whispering lover. Now even murder had lost that intimacy. Murder was done by moving away, by isolating, by leaving a colleague bleeding. Messages were not delivered face to face, but sent through unattributed quotes in the newspapers. Death was no more intimate now than ten seconds on the news.

The leadership did nothing to save Wright. Coelho's whip organization was dormant. Foley sat in the cloakroom, in his own reasoned way making Wright's case. But Wright was on his own. Whenever the rare positive story appeared some member circulated it with a Dear Colleague. But members had to be asked even to do that. One Wright aide said, "Nobody volunteers."

"Who's defending Wright?" said one friend. "Outside of the Texans, nobody. The closest is when you walk through the Speaker's Lobby—you can't even walk through, it's like a pack of wolves—reporters ask, 'What are you gonna do? What are you gonna do?' 'Can I see the evidence first?' you say. That's the closest to a defense."

A Harris poll concluded that a solid majority of Americans believed Wright should remain as Speaker unless found guilty.

Charlie Rangel called and told him he had to fight this. Wright said how could he, he had no support.

"How do you know?" Rangel replied. "You got anybody counting? How do you know what support you have? Who should I talk to? Marty Frost? Foley? Who?"

No one. There was no one to talk to. Rangel had waited to be asked. No one had asked. Wright knew members wanted to be asked. But he wouldn't ask for this. This was too personal. And it was over now.

When he walked onto the floor, into the cloakroom, members stiffened. There was an awkwardness. They could not talk about his difficulties with him. But what else could they talk about? Even these politicians, so skilled at charming even each other, so skilled at saying nothing, could only smile and cough. Even those who wished him well, even they... what could they say? They were waiting for him to go away. This was no longer his House.

Wright was walking through the Rayburn Building to a meeting. Gingrich was coming the other way down the corridor. They could not avoid each other. As they walked past, Wright, his smile fixed on his face, said, "Hey, Newt."

Gingrich said nothing, just silently watched him pass.

Almost two weeks had passed since the charges had been made. It seemed like two years. Only a trial would clear the air, prove his innocence, give him a chance to survive. The Ethics Committee would not schedule one, claiming it could not until it had concluded the investigation into the oil deal.

Wright snapped, "A pimp has more due process than I do."

The press mounted what they called the "death watch," complete with motorcycles which were impossible to lose. Over the Memorial Day weekend Wright escaped into the Shenandoah Valley. First he had to drive from Virginia into Washington, opposite his destination, and enter the House garage where police prevented the press from following; then he switched cars and drove out another entrance.

He went to a friend's country retreat. It was not much more than commuting distance from Washington but it seemed another world, filled only with the smells of fields, the view into the clean distance. It was warm. In the eighties. In the foreground was a barn, hay, some other works of men. Behind them he counted range after range of ancient mountains, so ancient that the world had worn them down to little more than hills. He counted within his view five distinct rings of mountains and imagined the five sets of valleys between them. There was not a sign of man in them, not that he could see, except for the barn immediately before him. He thought for a moment that for all one's ambitions, all one could do was change the foreground a little. He had done that already. He felt at peace, his decision made.

He would leave.

First he would speak on the House floor. It was what he had wanted for a year and a half. To take the floor and explain himself. That morning he wolfed down his breakfast. His hand was almost shaking. He finished abruptly and left; for the first time perhaps ever, he shouldered his way through the reporters staked outside the door with no comment of any kind.

By mid-afternoon the press gallery was full, crowded, more so than anyone could ever remember. There was, even in this age of nonsmokers, stale cigarette smoke in clouds in the room.

No Speaker in the nation's history had been forced from office. But all the forces Jim Wright had unleashed in the 100th Congress, all the forces in himself, had brought him to this point.

The lights of the House were turned up; the networks were televising Wright's speech live. The chamber was full. Not a member left the floor.

Wright strode to the well of the House, where he had spoken so many hundreds of times. "Mr. Speaker," he said to Foley, Speaker pro tem, who was in the chair, "I ask that I may be heard on a question of personal privilege."

"The distinguished Speaker is recognized for one hour."

"For thirty-four years," Wright began, "I have had the great privilege to be a member of this institution, the people's House, and I shall forever be grateful for that wondrous privilege.... And you, my colleagues— Democrats and Republicans—I owe a great deal. You have given me the greatest gift within your power to give. To be the Speaker of the U.S. House of Representatives is the grandest opportunity that can come to any lawmaker in the western world....I would hope that I have reflected credit upon the people of my district, who know me best, and upon the people of this House who, next to them, know me best."

Democrats applauded, as did scattered Republicans. Michel did not. The GOP leadership sat together, occupying one row, Gingrich, the new whip, next to Michel. It was a new Congress. Trent Lott had moved to the Senate, Dick Cheney had become secretary of defense, and Gingrich had beaten Michel's candidate by two votes to win the whip job. Wright reviewed the accomplishments of the 100th Congress and then said, "I love this institution. I want to assure each of you that under no circumstances, having spent more than half my life here, this House being my home, would I ever knowingly or intentionally do or say anything to violate its rules or detract from its standing....

"For nearly a year I have ached to tell my side of the story. Today silence is no longer tolerable, nor, for the good of the House, is it even desirable.... So without any rancor or bitterness, without any hard feeling toward anybody, I thank you for indulging me as I answer to you, and the American people, for my honor, my reputation, and all the things I tried to stand for all these years."

Now, finally, with his audience the American people, and not the media, he told his story for an hour. As he spoke, he turned. He mopped his brow. He wiped the sweat from his face. And he was compelling. He made his case powerfully, rebutting the charges point by point. There was an intensity in him, this man who was such a bad television performer, a riveting intensity which reached through the television and seized hold of people. This voice, so gently urgent. And he pleaded for the House.

"When vilification becomes an accepted form of political debate, when negative campaigning becomes a full-time occupation, when members of each party become self-appointed vigilantes carrying out personal vendettas against members of the other party, in God's name, that is not what this institution is about. . . . All of us, in both political parties, must resolve to bring this mindless cannibalism to an end. There has been enough of it.

"I pray to God we will do that and restore the spirit that always existed in the House."

He smiled. That smile that was so unkind to him and which he could not rid himself of. He put his hands on his hips.

"Have I made mistakes? Oh, boy. How many!

"If I have offended anybody in the other party, I am sorry. I never meant to. . . . Are there things I would do differently if I had them to do over again? Oh, boy, how many may I name for you?

"Well, I tell you what. Let me give you back this job you gave me as a propitiation for all of this season of bad will that has grown up among us. Let me give it back to you. I will resign as Speaker of the House effective upon the election of my successor, and I will ask that we call a Caucus on the Democratic side for next Tuesday to choose a successor.

"I do not want to be a party to tearing this institution up. I love it. . . . I will offer to resign from the House sometime before the end of June. Let that be a total payment for the anger and hostility we feel toward each other. . . . God bless this institution. God bless the United States."

What had Wright actually done? His wife clearly had done real work. But there was the book—$4,500 in royalties over three years that the committee questioned. Members of both parties who actually wrote the royalty rules agreed that the book did not violate any rules, that Wright had found a loophole. As usual, he had rammed his shoulder against the edge of the rules and made space for himself.

And yet, didn't the public rightly demand more? Hadn't Wright himself demanded more in those early years in politics? Hadn't Wright himself agreed that the Speaker of the House should be held to a higher standard than his colleagues? There were those who believed the book alone was enough to cost him his speakership. There were others who dismissed it as worth no more than one embarrassing editorial in normal times. But these weren't normal times, and Wright as much as Gingrich had created the abnormality.

Two years before Wright resigned, as Gingrich was launching his campaign against him, he had said, "If Wright survives this ethics thing, he may become the greatest Speaker since Henry Clay."

Gingrich had also said, "He creates himself when he acts. That's very threatening to a system governed by rules."

Gingrich was correct. Wright did act, and created new realities in doing so. There was smallness in him, too much smallness, but there was largeness too. Pushing the limits of his own personality, himself on edge, he put others on edge and seemed to personify the chaos not of what is possible—politics is the art of the possible—but of what might become possible. That potential chaos represented the best in him. There was power in him, and will, and the willingness to use power.

John Myers sat in his office, talking about the committee, justifying his votes, and asked, "Suppose instead of 'undue influence' the charge was 'abuse of power.' Wouldn't you vote for it then?"

There was no such charge. But was that why Myers had voted against Wright? For abusing power? How many other Republicans voted against him for abuse of power?

Whether Wright did abuse power or not, though, he had used it. And the committee used its, too.

A few days before Wright left Congress, Costa Rican President Oscar Arias wrote him a letter crediting him with bringing peace to Central America and thanking him. Arias won the Nobel Peace Prize for his own role in bringing that peace.

EPILOGUE

In the first chapter many pages ago, I said that this is a book about power in many of its incarnations. Some of what is contained in here came directly from my own experiences, some from my role as an journalist.

I always resisted being called a "journalist." My view of the profession was formed when I was a high school sophomore and got into a football game for the first time. The local paper published the names of everyone who got into the game, so the next morning I got up early to see my name in the paper. It wasn't there. Worse, someone with whom I competed and who had not played had his name in the paper. At the time I thought the papers must do a better job when they wrote about something important. Much later I discovered that, too often, the press was sloppy with important things too.

The press disappoints so much because in a free society it matters so much. It is not the role of the press to right wrongs, or even necessarily to uncover truths. That is too much to expect, given the competitive pressures driving the media—the need to be first, a fear of sticking out when wrong and of falling behind when everyone else in moving in another direction—which makes it superficial and headline-oriented. One cannot even expect it to resist particularly well being manipulated, since it often serves the media's own interest to yield to manipulation. But one can expect it to correct lies, and to report truths uncovered by society's critics. And one can expect less smugness and self-congratulation, and more self-examination and self-criticism. That much is possible because it requires only a change of fashion, not a change in the institution. Gingrich didn't invent negative campaigning or personal attacks. Andrew Jackson's morals were a matter of public debate, until he killed one critic in a duel. Grover Cleveland's morals were part of a presidential campaign ("Ma, Ma, where's my pa?/ Gone to the White House, ha, ha, ha"). Supreme Court nominee Robert Bork's views, though not him personally, were attacked in a conscious and concerted manner.

But Gingrich's calculated, purposeful media campaign against that "useful keystone to a much larger structure," as he himself called the Speaker of the House, was less justified on the facts, more methodical, more directed, more conscious than any before it, and it used the purely personal to advance the purely political. Even Joe McCarthy had limited himself to accusing—accurately or not—his victims of holding leftist policy positions.

Gingrich succeeded and launched a politics of vitriol. He repeated it and others copied it. I am no admirer of Clarence Thomas, probably the weakest Supreme Court justice and certainly the least-deserving of nomination in my lifetime, but the accusations involving his personal behavior had no business being explored by a Senate committee.

But, Thomas notwithstanding, Republicans have pursued this line of personal vitriol far more than the Democrats. Soon after the Lewinsky scandal broke Gingrich said he would never make another speech without mentioning it.

Such personal attacks have not always paid off. After the dismal GOP showing in the 1998 election, Gingrich's colleagues suggested he leave the Speakership, even though he had led them to power in the House for the first time in forty years. Ironically, Bob Livingston did the asking, he who had rejected Gingrich's package of charges against Wright as insufficient. Livingston stepped briefly to the front as the Speaker-designate, only to be brought down in a matter of days by his own scandal. (Perhaps the greatest irony was that, just as Gingrich had his own embarrassing book deals while he was attacking Wright, he also had his own affair with a younger staff person while he was attacking Clinton. No one said Gingrich didn't have guts.)

In politics, the mindless cannibalism that Wright decried goes on. But it has not always triumphed. Perhaps it has already run its course. That depends on the voter more than the media.

The media of course will always put controversy on the front page, even while individual journalists bemoan it and resist what is happening. It is the nature of the beast.

Allow me to make some final comments about the media and about power.

There are some excellent journalists. They have the opportunity not just to meet but often to know an extraordinary array of people. The word "know" is appropriate because many journalists do sometimes spend considerable time learning about and studying people and issues. For me, that was almost always the case since I never did daily journalism, never covered a breaking story, never had to "make do," never had to throw something together on deadline before I knew much about it. For most of my roughly ten years as a Washington journalist, I wrote full-length magazine pieces and spent anywhere from a few weeks to several months researching a single story. I had the opportunity to learn. I never had to resist the pressures my former colleagues felt constantly.

I also had good fortune in three other ways.

My first piece of good fortune was to have a brilliant model that rarely left my thoughts, especially when writing about an individual. That model was Samuel Johnson's *An Account of the Life of Richard Savage,* which seemed absolutely relentless in pursuit of the truth and yet sympathetic to his close friend Savage. That was how I tried to approach my subjects— relentlessly but sympathetically. (Take note, however, that Richard Holmes demonstrated in his book *Johnson and Savage* that Johnson wrote rather less truth than he knew.)

Second, I made a mistake early in my career, which cut down on my arrogance and taught me not to take anything for granted. The issue itself was trivial. I was profiling Jerry Claiborne for the *Washington Post.* Claiborne then coached football at the University of Maryland, whose team had just finished an undefeated regular season ranked fourth in the country. Claiborne had played for Bear Bryant and coached in that mold: an Old Testament paternalistic type, he loved you, but you better do it his way. Team rules included rigid dress codes, dismissal from the team for having a beer, no facial hair, and the like. His players called him "the bone" because he was so hard, and because the nickname had sexual innuendo—they thought he screwed them. My mistake lay in misinterpreting his relationship with his son, who started for that team but had walked on—i.e., he had tried out for the team without a scholarship. Few "walk-ons" ever get to play at all, much less start for one of the nation's best teams. I had imagined a father-son relationship in which the son was determined to prove his worthiness, his character, his toughness to his father. I had imagined a clash of wills. Journalists joke, "never let the facts ruin a good story." In this case the facts did ruin the story. A little reporting showed that they were far warmer and loving toward one another than I had thought. After that I made sure that my reporting came first, my interpretations second.

Third, because I did not cover stories dictated by events, I had to come up with story ideas myself, and therefore usually wrote about what interested me. No journalist who considers himself or herself serious enjoys staking out the house of people in trouble and jamming a microphone in their face, and few enjoy covering personal scandals at all. I never had to do anything like that. It is far more fun to research something that interests you, especially when you came up with the idea yourself, than not.

So writing gave me some phenomenal chances to observe at close hand many people considered powerful. These included not only many congressional leaders and three Speakers of the House, but several Presidents of the United States and several chiefs of state (I even got the chance to watch Mikhail Gorbachev at the peak of his power operate backstage), along with religious figures, business chief executives, even several Nobel laureate scientists. Add to that the normal experiences of life that anyone has—in my case that means especially my sports background, which brought me into close contact with two men named national football coach of the year, a dozen pro football players, and four world record-holding athletes—and I have been exposed to a disparate set of leaders.

I hope I learned something about power. To me, power seems white, blank; a great white slick surface, abstract, ungiving, impersonal, objective. One can *feel* it. As I noted earlier, in Washington lights shining on the Capitol make the white marble luminescent and visible for miles. Cold radiates from the immense, thick sandstone columns, great large blocks of stone and marble, cool even in summer. One stands there and feels the chill of power. Like love, it is icy to those without. Like love, it chooses and, ultimately, makes no compromise. Like love, it brooks no rival.

Power resists. At its core it yields nothing. And of course it imposes itself. Powerful people almost by definition impose themselves, and their visions, upon the world.

Usually they evidence great ambition, but there are many ways to exercise power.

Two people come to mind who represent extreme examples of opposite styles, yet both changed at least part of the world. The most focused person I have ever met was Mother Theresa. There was nothing soft about her, and she seemed to me almost ruthless. You did not want to get in her way. Yet Cardinal Paulo Evaristo Arns, a major social and political figure in Brazil, had the softness of a lamb and carried with him all the power of softness, sort of like Muhammed Ali's rope-a-dope, when he leaned against the ropes and let George Foreman hit him until Foreman exhausted himself.

The ambition of many politicians and truly serious athletes sound grand. Some build empires. Some try to change the world, affect the course of events. Some strive to leave the largest possible mark upon the world. Nehemiah left track for several mediocre years in the NFL, but in 1997 was inducted into the Track and Field Hall of Fame. At his induction he said, "Pro football opened the door for me to show another form of my athletic prowess. It has taken me seventeen years to put the Olympic Games in perspective. That was a hollow feeling. The induction has made up for that. . . . I was obsessed with being the best. . . . Now, I see they regard me as the all-time greatest hurdler. I am able to appreciate that. My greatest accomplishment is my induction. It's the exclamation point to my career. This is my gold medal."

Few sound as candid as Nehemiah about their need for acclaim. But many want what he wanted.

Yet there are seemingly smaller ambitions that are actually bigger. I think of a friend who is neither a politician nor an athlete. Indeed, he hasn't played an organized sport since Little League (although he was an all-star second baseman back then, and he does keep his bat from those days around his apartment). When he was still in school I asked him what his ambition in life was. He told me it was "to be civilized."

His goal certainly does sound modest and conjures up images of cafes and opera, but he actually meant a large and deep thing. He intended to live in a quiet yet uncompromising way that affected everything he touched in his life. This requires courage, and imposing a kind of civilization upon the world around him. I believe he has done so with considerable tenacity.

His ambition reminds me of something Emerson wrote: "to throw him on his resources, and tax the strength of his character... to demonstrate to all men that there is intelligence and good will at the heart of things, and ever higher and yet higher leadings... and for solace the perspective of your own infinite life; and for work the study and communication of principles, the making those instincts prevalent, the conversion of the world."

The difference between Nehemiah's feelings and that of this friend is akin to the distinction between dignity and pride discussed in the first chapter; one depends upon the individual's view of himself or herself, the other on the world's view of the individual.

But each of the different vantage points resemble each other in one thing: they can transform the individual into a force.

How then do individuals exercise force?

Some can do so as simply as being themselves. But because something is simple does not mean it is not difficult. Rosa Parks comes to mind.

Others, chiefly empire builders, need more.

In addition to having a vision and will that can precipitate order out of chaos, can crystallize a particular reality out of the possibilities that already exist, those who achieve much, whether they are athletes or civilizers or writers or imperialists, routinely do one other thing: they risk everything.

This willingness to risk everything, and commit oneself completely, itself represents another kind of power.

Jim Wright risked everything and disappeared from public life; few people even recall his name, or that he ever served as Speaker. Yet he did redirect the nation's domestic policy and made a major contribution to peace in Central America. Newt Gingrich risked destroying himself by attacking Wright and ultimately won for the Republican Party control of the House for the first time in forty years.

The athletes risked themselves as well, poured all of their minds and bodies into their sport, and faced failure in ways few others do. I could say what each of them is doing today. I don't want to. Not all of them have led fortunate lives. One athlete I later became quite friendly with graduated from college with tremendous renown from success in football, yet briefly became homeless.

I haven't talked to him in ten years. The last time we spoke, he called me collect late at night. He needed money. $1,218, half what he owed someone, to keep them from prosecuting him for passing bad checks.

I promised him the money. We talked for a long time. He said that he had never had to really work to achieve success athletically, that he had tried a few things after sports, but that he had never wanted to face reality and deal with the world.

I felt and he probably felt that he had become a ghost.

He said he hated athletics now. He hadn't realized how superficial it was. It had been his whole identity. He said the only job he had ever gotten on his own was pumping gas.

So I will not update those in this book. I prefer to think of the athletes and even of the politicians in here at their best: breaking tackles, thrusting their chests across the finish line, making a peace. I prefer to think of them reaching and stretching, if too often failing. And so I think also of Auden's "Musee des Beaux Arts,"

> In Bruegel's Icarus, for instance: how everything turns away
> Quite leisurely from the disaster; the ploughman may
> Have heard the splash, the forsaken cry,
> But for him it was not an important failure, the sun shone
> As it had to on the white legs disappearing into the green
> Water; and the expensive delicate ship that must have seen
> Something amazing, a boy falling out of the sky,
> Had somewhere to get to and sailed calmly on.

INDEX

Abrams, Elliot, 96
Anderson, Jack, 189
Anthony, Beryl, 143
Arias, Oscar, 94, 97, 98, 201
Arns, Paulo Evaristo, 207
Atkins, Chester, 186
AuCoin, Les, 110

Babcock, Charles, 47, 134, 144, 193–94
Baker, James, 47–49
Baltimore Sun, 49
Barnes, Marvin, 15
Bednarski, Bob, 8, 169
Black Caucus, 107–08, 112–13
Bonior, David, 35, 94, 109, 120–21, 125
Bork, Robert, 204
Boston Globe, 49, 146
Bowen, Otis, 90–91
Bradlee, Ben, 50, 133–34
Brinkley, Joel, 95
Broder, David, 147
Brooks, Jack, 30, 104
Brown University, 11, 15, 16
Bryant, Bear, 205
Bush, George, Sr., 47, 48, 50, 102, 142, 146–47, 148
Bush, George W., Jr., 48–49
Butcher, Willard, 135

Cameron, Mark, 168–74
Canetti, Elias, 51–52, 196
Carter, Amon, 28

Carter, Jimmy, 50, 52, 175
Cassidy, Gerald, 188
Chapman, Jim, 117, 118, 119–21, 122
Cheney, Dick, 34, 92, 105, 125–26, 129, 140, 147, 196, 199
Choyke, William, 48
Claiborne, Jerry, 205–06
Cleveland, Grover, 204
Clinton, Bill, 50, 108, 204
Cochran, Johnnie, 133
Coelho, Tony, 35, 41, 89, 90, 103–05, 107–08, 109–10, 112–13, 114, 117, 119–20, 125, 140, 144, 197
Common Cause, 41, 93, 135, 141, 143, 145, 146, 191
Congressional Quarterly, 128
Connell, Mary Wright, 24, 25
Conservative Opportunity Society, 37, 39, 43
Costello, Frank, 155
Cronkite, Walter, 50

Dallas Times-Herald, 195
Dannemyer, William, 115
Deaver, Michael, 40, 139
Detroit News, 51
Dingell, John, 90–91, 110
Dixon, Julian, 146, 179, 180–81, 183, 188, 192, 193, 194–95
Dole, Robert, 39, 102
Donaldson, Sam, 48
Donovan, Raymond, 40

Doyle, James, 51, 196
Dragan, Linda, 158–62
Duarte, Napoleón, 94
Dukakis, Michael, 146, 148
Dunham, Richard, 195
duPont, John, 163

Eckhardt, Bob, 32
Edwards, Mickey, 121–22
Eisenhower, Dwight, 30, 37
Ellender, Benny, 59, 76
Ethics Committee, 133, 138, 139,
    141, 145–46, 147, 148–49, 177,
    179–96, 198, 201

Farmer, Dave, 61
Fazio, Vic, 186, 187, 191
Ferreli, Gerry, 169
Fiedler, Tom, 136–37
Foley, Tom, 87–88, 89, 92, 97, 102,
    103, 107, 112, 113–14, 115, 118,
    123, 140, 144, 197, 199
Ford, Bill, 120
Ford, Gerald, 50, 51, 102, 103
Ft. McNair, 158
Fort Worth Star-Telegram, 48, 193–94
Fort Worth, Tex., 30
Fox, Edward, 98
Frank, Barney, 105
Frankfurter, Felix, 86–87
Frazier, Joe, 30
Frisby, Owen, 135
Frost, Martin, 120, 197
Fund, John, 144–45

Gaubert, Thomas, 182
Gaydos, Joe, 186, 187
Gaylord, Joseph, 42
Gergen, David, 140
Germond, Jack, 49
Gingrich, Newt, 5, 19, 20, 33, 35–
    44, 46, 47, 52–53, 83, 85, 93, 99,
    121, 124, 125, 126, 128–29, 131,
    133–49, 177, 179, 189, 191, 197,
    199, 201, 203–04, 208

Goldwater, Barry, 37
Good Morning, America, 94–95,
    128, 139
Gorbachev, Mikhail, 126, 206
Gore, Al, 49
Gray, Bill, 112–13
Gray, Boyden, 47–48
Greene, Graham, 24
Greenfield, Meg, 134
Gutman, Roy, 96

Halberstam, David, 47
Halleck, Charles, 123
Hansen, James, 188
Harvey, Paul, 135
Hawkins, Gus, 112
Hersh, Seymour, 47
House of Ill Repute, A, 43
Howell, Lee, 36
Howlett, Michael, Jr., 187
Hubbard, Carl, 60
Hughes, Judy, 146
Hunt, Al, 195
Hutcheson, Ron, 193

Jackson, Alvin, 7
Jackson, Andrew, 203–04
Jackson, Brooks, 48, 134, 145, 195
James, Lee, 172
Jeffords, Jim, 121
Johnson, Lyndon, 30, 50, 104
Johnson, Samuel, 205

Kemp, Jack, 144
Kenworthy, Thomas, 195
Kilpatrick, James, 142
Koppel, Ted, 133, 146, 147
Kovach, Bill, 5

Laghi, Pio, 127
Leahy, Nancy, 160
Leath, Marvin, 90, 107
Lemmons, Mary Ethelyn "Mab,"
    24, 28, 29, 30–31

Lewinsky, Monica, 204
Lewis, Kirk, 61
Livingston, Robert, 141–42, 144, 148, 149, 204
Loeffler, Tom, 93–94, 95, 97
Los Angeles Times, 49, 50, 146
Lott, Trent, 35, 89, 94, 112, 120, 121, 125, 140, 199
Lowry, Mike, 92, 120
Lucas, Wingate, 28
Lynam, Marshall, 147

Mack, John, 87, 95, 105, 108, 112, 113, 118, 120, 179
MacKay, Buddy, 89, 90
MacNeil-Lehrer show, 146
Madigan, Ed, 115, 121
Mallick, George, 182–83, 184–86, 190, 192
Mallightco, 182, 184–86, 191, 193–94
Martin, Joe, 122–23
Maryland, University of, 154, 171, 173
McCarthy, Joe, 40, 204
McCormick, John, 20, 30
Meese, Edwin, 41, 47, 140–41, 146–47
Miami Herald, 136–37
Micahnik, Dave, 165
Michel, Bob, 111, 113–14, 117, 119, 123–24, 125, 128, 140, 141, 199
Miller, Eugene, 26–27
Miller, George, 89, 114, 115, 118
Miller, Jay, 60
Miller, Karl, 172
Mills, Joe, 8, 169, 170, 173
Mollohan, Alan, 185–86, 192
Moody, Jim, 120
Morro, Al, 6–7, 81
Mother Theresa, 207
Mussolini, Benito, 38
Myers, John, 180, 183, 189, 192, 193, 194–95, 201

Nader, Ralph, 140–41
Natcher, William, 91
Nehemiah, Renaldo, 153–57, 207
New Republic, 146
New York Times, 5, 45, 47, 49, 50, 51, 95–96, 97, 140, 142, 146, 148, 193, 194, 196
New York Times Magazine, 4
Newsday, 96
Newsweek, 49, 51, 134, 137, 141, 189, 196
Nicaragua, 93–98, 126, 127–29
Nightline, 146
Nixon, Richard, 50
Nofziger, Lyn, 40, 139

Obando y Bravo, Miguel, 127–28
Obey, David, 194
Oldaker, Bill, 179, 181, 183, 184, 188, 190–91, 192
O'Neill, Tip, 19, 32, 38, 84, 87, 106, 113, 126, 139–40
Ornstein, Norman, 83, 133
Ortega, Daniel, 37, 127–29
Osborne, David, 36

Pashayan, Chip, 191, 192
Payte, Gene, 194, 195
Pena, Richard, 94
Pennsylvania, University of, 163
Penny, Tim, 90, 110
Petri, Thomas, 186, 189–90
Phelan, Richard, 180–96
Plunkett, Jim, 57
Providence, R.I., 6, 11

Rahall, Nick, 117
Rangel, Charlie, 112–13, 197
Raupe, Craig, 29, 32–33
Rayburn, Sam, 85, 106, 122–23
Reagan, Ronald, 35, 37, 39, 47, 50, 88, 91, 93–94, 95, 97, 98, 99, 102, 126, 127, 139, 144, 147–48, 175

Reed, Thomas, 125
Reflections of a Public Man, 134
Regardie's, 137–38, 139, 189
Rhodes, John, 40
Richardson, Bill, 116, 124
Ridenhour, Rod, 47
Roberts, Steve, 95–96
Rockefeller, Nelson, 37
Roemer, Buddy, 110
Rogers, David, 195–96
Rohatyn, Felix, 103
Roosevelt, Franklin, 20, 25
Rosenthal, Abe, 140
Rostenkowski, Dan, 32, 100, 101, 107, 108–09, 119
Rules Committee, 100–01, 112
Russo, Marty, 87, 108, 109, 114–15, 119, 120, 122

Sadat, Anwar, 42
St. Germain, Fernand, 133, 195
Sawyer, Harold, 194
Schneider, Claudine, 88–89
Sensenbrenner, James, 141, 142, 144, 148
Sevareid, Eric, 49
Shultz, George, 94, 126, 128
Sixty Minutes, 133
Smith, Dick, 173
Smith, Pamela, 185, 191
Sorzano, José, 96
Speakes, Larry, 48
Stark, Fortney "Pete," 118
Stenholm, Charles, 89–90, 101–02, 105–06, 107, 109, 110, 116, 138
Storm, Michael, 163–67
Strauss, Bob, 143
Swillinger, Daniel, 142
Swindall, Patrick, 143
Swirz, Adam, 172–73

Tauk, Tom, 137
ter Horst, Jerry, 51
Texas, University of, 26

Thayer, Paul, 40
Thomas, Clarence, 204
Thompson, Bobby, 15
Thompson, Ernest, 25
Time, 49, 133
Tulane University, 8, 58, 65–66, 76–79

US News and World Report, 49, 140

Van Brocklin, Karen, 137, 140, 142, 145

Walker, Robert, 42, 115, 116
Wall Street Journal, 45, 48, 49, 50, 108, 133, 137, 140, 144–46, 193, 195
Wanniski, Jude, 144
Washington, Harold, 109
Washington Post, 45, 47, 49, 50, 51, 128, 133–34, 137, 140, 141, 142, 144, 145, 146, 147, 193–94, 195, 196, 205
Washington Times, 49, 141
Waxman, Henry, 91
Weatherford, Tex., 22, 27
Weld, William, 41, 142
Wertheimer, Fred, 41–42, 93, 141, 143, 144, 145–46
White, John, 143
Will, George, 142
Williams, Pat, 92
Wilson, Woodrow, 26
Window of Opportunity, 138
Wright, Betty Hay (wife), 29, 126, 184–85, 186, 190–91, 192, 193, 200
Wright, Betty Lee (sister), 24
Wright, James "Jim," 4–5, 19, 20, 21–35, 36, 37, 38, 41–44, 47, 48, 83–95, 97–129, 131, 133–48, 177, 179, 180, 181–201, 208

Zumbach, Dave, 61